"In my Hollywood days, I was cast in n   roles in TV, stage, and films. But never   ate, humble, and driven to fulfill the pla   in mind for me as I am today. Our Creator is the ultimate casting agent, but we have to 'show up' for the part. We must choose to audition, and if we pursue, we'll find that we are uniquely suited for the role God has written just for us. In reading Lucinda Secrest McDowell's *Role of a Lifetime*, you'll be blessed with a coach to inspire and support you along the way to your destiny. God knows the full potential *He* has placed in each of us, and based on His Word, Cindy will cheer you on with insight and direction to that end. Applause, applause!"

— **Jennifer O'Neill**
    Actress, Author, Speaker
    www.jenniferoneill.com

"Lights! Camera! . . . What? No 'action'? If you have ever stood on the stage of your life wondering, *If all the world's a stage, why can't I get a better storyline?* then you are holding the right book in your hands. In *Role of a Lifetime* Cindy challenges us to examine our past, embrace our present, and embark on new journeys that will lead us to live fully. Prepare to find yourself immersed in the role you were always destined to play."

— **Anita Renfroe**
    Comedian, Author, Songwriter,
    Women of Faith Speaker, www.anitarenfroe.com

"Thank you, Cindy! As a drama queen, I love knowing I'm a daughter of THE drama King. Inviting us to view the wonder in our lives, *Role of a Lifetime* sings a song of worth and validity for all who need to know they are not just marking time this side of heaven. With elegance you have turned the tables on a culture that misses the value of lives lived behind the scene. In this beautiful work, you show us that all stories are profound because all lives are uniquely treasured."

— **Bonnie Keen**
    Recording Artist, Author, and Speaker
    www.bonniekeen.com

"In the words of the great political reformer William Wilberforce, Lucinda Secrest McDowell challenges the reader to 'boldly assert the call of Christ in an age, where so many who bear the name of Christian are ashamed of Him.' Through her delightful story-telling and spiritual truths, Cindy illustrates in *Role of a Lifetime* how we can integrate faith into the roles God has called us to— from the pulpit, the stage, in the home . . . wherever we are."

— **Ken and Susan Wales**
  Authors and Producers of *Amazing Grace* movie,
  Christy CBS series, and the annual *Movieguide*® awards

"Have you been wandering around aimlessly wondering what your actual role on this earth is supposed to be? In a clarifying, encouraging style, Lucinda Secrest McDowell gives you that answer as she wraps her arms around you and reveals exactly what you are here for! As someone whose career was placing people in coveted roles in the film and television industry, I know how essential it is to discover your Life Role rather than merely a temporary role after temporary role. Filled with wisdom, insight, instruction, laughter, and tears, *Role of a Lifetime* is sure to give you many 'Aha' moments. I loved this book. Buy it; grab a pen; and journal your way to your role of a lifetime."

— **Victorya Michaels Rogers**
  Author, Relationship Coach,
  and Former Hollywood Agent

"*Role of a Lifetime: Your Part in God's Story* by Lucinda (Cindy) Secrest McDowell provides wonderful faith-affirming insights that will help you deal victoriously with the trials and tribulations of real life. Built on the firm foundation of Scripture, her book uses some elements of reel life to illuminate real life."

— **Ted Baehr**
  Founder and Publisher of *Movieguide*®
  Chairman of the Christian Film
  & Television Commission

role of a
lifetime

role of a
lifetime

your part in God's Story

lucinda secrest mcdowell

B&H
PUBLISHING GROUP

nashville, tennessee

ISBN: 978-0-8054-4662-3

Published by B&H Publishing Group,
Nashville, Tennessee

Dewey Decimal Classification: 248.843
Subject Heading: CHRISTIAN LIFE \ WOMEN

Unless otherwise noted, all Scripture quotations are taken from the Holman Christian Standard Bible® copyright © 1999, 2000, 2002, 2003 by Holman Bible Publishers. Used by permission. Holman Christian Standard Bible®, Holman CSB®, and HCSB® are federally registered trademarks of Holman Bible Publishers.

Other Bibles quoted are marked CEV, Contemporary English Version, copyright © 1995 by American Bible Society; MSG, The Message, copyright © 1993, 1994, 1995, 1996, 2000, 2001, 2002 by Eugene H. Peterson; NIV, New International Version, copyright © 1973, 1978, 1984 by International Bible Society.

In quotations throughout this book, the author often uses italics for emphasis, which may or may not be part of the original texts.

2 3 4 5 6 7 8 9 10 11 12 13 14 15   12 11 10 09 08

Dedicated to my four children:

Justin Thomas Gregory McDowell
Timothy Michael Laurens McDowell
Fiona Johanna Yvonne McDowell
Margaret Sarah Secrest McDowell

*May each of you continue to embrace
your unique and adventurous role in God's kingdom story.
And may God, who loves you even more than I do,
grant you grace, gratitude, and glorious victory
in your own life story.*

Contents

Confessions of a Drama Queen

We can serve within who God made us to be;
We can live out the dream He's put in our hearts.
—Keri Wyatt Kent, *Listen*

When I was eight years old, I landed the role of a lifetime. I was asked to be the, ahem, *princess* in our third-grade production of "The Frog Prince." And before you ask, yes, I did have to kiss the frog. Nonetheless, I was over the moon when casting was announced. What little girl doesn't want to be a princess? The previous year, in second grade, I had played merely one of the many elves in "The Shoemaker and the Elves." Frog or no frog, this princess gig had to be better than that. Think of the costume possibilities alone . . .

Not only did I get to wear a rhinestone tiara, but Mama remade an old ball gown with a huge white net skirt covered with silver sequins into my princess costume. I sang at least two solos, the lyrics of which I remember to this day. I was, as they say, in my element.

Today, remembering this childhood event, I can make at least three observations that reveal not only the person I was but also the story I was to live out in years to come:

1. I was perfectly at ease on stage with a microphone in front of an audience of hundreds. (Amazingly enough, I have spent most of my adult life as a professional speaker to large groups of people.)
2. Being part of communicating a story with a moral or lesson was meaningful to me, and I loved doing it. (As an author, I share the truth and hope of God's Word and how it practically applies to our lives today.)
3. Having the lead role gave me a sense of achievement that, in turn, made me feel worthy; therefore, I deliberately began pursuing more achievements. (One of my greatest spiritual and emotional struggles as an adult has been the need to be released from striving too much and attempting to find my worth in doing rather than being.)

Recently someone called me a drama queen, and I don't think she even knew about "The Frog Prince." I'm pretty sure it wasn't a compliment. A dictionary defines that slang phrase: "melodramatic person: somebody who likes to make a drama out of a situation by acting in an emotional way." Well, you don't have to get snippy about it! OK, OK, so I'm emotional, although I can be plenty cerebral when I want to. That's who I am. I prefer to define myself as a person who embraces life to the fullest—in an effusive sort of way, of course. My motto is "If it's worth doing, it's worth doing with *flair!*"

Drama queen or not, we all play roles in life. Some are roles of our choosing, those we have envisioned from the time we could dream of our futures and picture ourselves there (bride, brain surgeon, or country music singer—you fill in the blanks). Other roles are those we never would have auditioned for and would just as well have passed over (prodigal daughter, divorcée, or cancer patient).

But God doesn't want His children merely to play roles, like putting on one hat one day and another the next. He loves us so much that He chose to create each of us in the image of His Son, Jesus Christ, and to infuse us with unique gifts and abilities that, when offered back to Him, would be used to help further His kingdom here on earth. We are a big deal to Him, and, therefore, we are cast in the role of a lifetime, one that truly matters—beloved servant of the Most High God.

Will you accept that role? You know you want to. You've been living one life while longing for another, and things aren't getting any better, are they? You're immersed in small stories and wonder why you can't find meaning in your madness. Merely keeping rules and embracing a system of beliefs is not enough anymore. And you're really tired of kissing frogs.

All Christ followers long to be part of what God is doing in the universe. We know He is building a kingdom, and we secretly wonder if there might be a role for us to play in that process. Could we really be princes and princesses destined to reign with Him? Dare we envision a life in which our everyday choices matter for all eternity? Where battles are fought and won because we were willing to venture forth in courage to uphold Truth? Do our lives matter?

While none of us can count our days left on earth, we can all make sure our days on earth count for something greater.

- If you are weary of worrying and burdened by busyness, then perhaps it's time to *change your life*.
- If you are preoccupied with the past and fearful of the future, then perhaps it's time to *choose a new life*.
- If you are ready to relinquish and are prepared to persevere, then it's definitely time to *know that you have a significant part in God's kingdom story*.

Step into this story, and let's discover our roles of a life-time together, relying on the incomparable power and presence of God Himself, the Author and Finisher of our faith.

Chapter 1

The Greatest Story Ever Told

We are made to live in God's Story . . . for God's glory . . .
with God's joy. It is only within *God's* Story that *our* stories find
their true meaning and destiny. . . . Though we spend much of life
relegating God to bit parts in our little autobiographies of
self-fulfillment, God generously "enfolds" us into His cosmic Story
of transforming love! Could any of us possibly want or hope
for more out of life? We are called into a story that *enfolds our own
stories in a grander narrative—*a story that is *going somewhere,
a story that is taking us with it.*
—Scotty Smith, *Restoring Broken Things*

D addy, please tell us a story!" we begged.
We had just finished another supper of corn bread,
Georgia field peas, baked ham, fresh sliced tomatoes and, of
course, sweet iced tea. My sisters and I had cleared the dishes,
and now came the time we eagerly awaited as we sat at the
family table. Which one would it be? The one about great-
grandfather Pratt, an inventor who had the first car in Atlanta
and kept the formula for Coca-Cola in his safe? Or the one
about Daddy's childhood pet frog, Puddin', who croaked so
long and loudly one night that Grandfather up and shot him?
Maybe we'd hear again of how Daddy, at age sixteen, wrote

the manager of the Waldorf-Astoria Hotel in New York City
and offered his high school band, *The Stardusters,* to play
there, receiving a very polite letter declining the offer. We
didn't care which one he chose. We loved a good story, and
Daddy told the best.

We also had family devotions around the table, from an
old green book whose title I regrettably can't recall now. From
that we heard other stories—of God's great love for a people
who too often rejected Him, of saints and sinners all used by
God to do incredible things, and of miracles, mangers, and
meanderings through the wilderness. And some nights Daddy
pulled out his reel-to-reel tape recorder and thrust the microphone in our faces, "interviewing" us about life, our school
activities, and, oh yes, our latest Bible memory verse. We
recited poetry and sang songs, and I, even from age two (I
know because I've heard the tape over and over again through
the years), kept trying to hog the mike. To this day, all of the
grandchildren love mocking their mamas' responses in those
long-ago interviews. They mimic our sweet Southern accents
and endless lists of what we hoped Santa would bring, not to
mention the sing-song poetry and our dramatic paraphrasing
of the first Christmas story.

Is it any wonder that I grew up loving stories? I still do.
Not only that, I'm grateful to be living a story, one that is
totally unique and utterly unpredictable. But most of all,
I rejoice that I'm part of God's great story of a kingdom that
never ends. It is my deepest prayer that I will fulfill the role
He has designed for me and be faithful to the end.

The world today is also enchanted with stories. We not
only want to read a good book or watch a thrilling movie; we
often become totally absorbed in the characters—both fic-
tional and real. We're eager to see the plot resolved, journey
completed, mystery solved, or lovers reconciled. Stories help

us deal with life. Author Madeleine L'Engle wrote her first story at age five: "I knew that it was through story that I was able to make some small sense of the confusions and complications of life. . . . I was frightened and I tried to heal my fear with stories which gave me courage, stories which affirmed that ultimately love is stronger than hate."[1]

Christ's followers are no different. Christians long for meaning in our ministry, purpose in our passion, and worth in our walk of faith. Preachers often use the power of storytelling to effect change and generate interest in pursuing the life of faith. Someone once called Jesus "a theologian who told stories." Eternal truths were communicated clearly through parables structured around everyday experiences, such as planting seeds, borrowing money, or welcoming home a rebellious teenager.

In my own speaking and teaching I've discovered that what the audience remembers most are my stories, which illustrate the points of each message. These flesh out biblical truth by drawing them into a familiar experience. Through this process an important "connect" is made: *If God can give Cindy the courage (or faith or hope or grace) in that situation, surely He can do the same for me!*

Singer Steven Curtis Chapman observed that we are becoming a narrative nation—people starving for the authenticity of personal story. "Instead of testimonies, we are learning to *share our stories*. Instead of the old-school, three-point sermon, pastors are developing *narrative preaching* styles. Instead of getting together with friends for a chat or just to hang out, we meet at Starbucks to *update our stories*. In the age-old continuum of 'show and tell,' our culture seems to be crying for a lot more *showing* (inviting) and a lot less *telling* (indicting)."[2]

It is my personal observation that in the twenty-first century people don't want to merely *read* stories or *watch* stories or even *tell* stories. They want to *live* stories. There is in each of us an innate desire to have a role to play—a major part in the saga that is life. And though most of us merely muddle through our days juggling responsibilities and relationships mired in the mundane, we desire more.

We want the magnificent.

A Story to *Know*

In *Walk the Line*, the biographical movie about the lives of Johnny and June Cash, young Johnny Cash (known at the time as J. R.) and his brother Jack are talking as they fall into bed after a hard hot day of picking cotton. J. R. wonders why Jack seems to be so good at everything.

"You pick five times more than me."

"Well, I'm bigger than you," Jack replies.

"But you know every story in Scriptures," J. R. protests.

"You know every song in Mama's hymnal."

"That's not the same. Songs are easy."

"Not for me," says Jack.

"There's more words in the Bible than 'Heavenly Highway Hymns,'" replies J. R.

"If I'm gonna be a preacher, I gotta know the Bible."

"Front to back?" J. R. questioned.

"You can't help somebody if you can't tell them the right story," Jack says emphatically.

Soon after that, Jack dies in a tragic accident, and Johnny grows up and goes to make his first record singing a gospel song. He seems to have a lifelong need to fulfill some of his late brother's dreams. And while his performance is technically correct, it ends up sounding like every other gospel recording. When asked why he won't record it, the record company executive says, "'Cause I don't believe you." While Johnny is trying to figure out if the man doesn't think he believes in the gospel he's singing about, the executive explains that he didn't sing it with passion.

"If you was hit by a truck and lying in the gutter dying and there was time to sing one song, one song people will remember before you're dirt, one song that tells God what you thought about your time here on earth, one song that sums up what you are; are you telling me that's what you'd sing? Hmmm. The same thing everyone sings? You'd sing about silver spray of rivers you never saw and saints gathering in misty places you never been? Or would you sing about something you felt. Something you touched. 'Cause, I'll tell you now, that's the kind of song people want to hear. That's the kind of song that saves people. It don't have nothing to do with believing in God, Mr. Cash. It has to do with believing in yourself."

Johnny thinks for a moment, and then sings an original gritty song from his heart. It's a story he knows because he has lived it. Needless to say, this performance lands him his first deal with Sun Records. And the rest is history.[3]

For our lives to make a difference in God's kingdom, we need to not only know the story and get it right, but we need to commit all our time and energy communicating from our hearts the things that truly matter—as though it were the last thing we would ever say.

Do you know God's story? How can we embrace our part in it if we haven't a clue what's going on? I'm continually amazed at the lack of knowledge of even the basics of the gospel story. In a recent Sunday newspaper, I came across an article on why parents should offer religious education to their children. The journalist, Gaile Robinson, began by recounting an outing to an old mission she had been on with her son's Scout troop:

The 200-year-old church was dark; in the gloom of the long, narrow sanctuary, the pews were barely visible. The only illumination was at the far end over the altar. There, a bright light spilled down over a huge crucifix and a larger-than-life wounded Christ figure, blood dripping from underneath the crown of thorns. The Cub Scouts were awed and, for a brief moment, silent.

Then, this query: "Whoa, what happened to that guy?"

I recognized the loud voice of my son at the same instant I experienced one of those whiplashes of profound parental guilt: "Oops, should have gotten the kids some religious education."

It had been on the to-do list, somewhere after toilet training and instructions on table manners; we just hadn't gotten to that particular chapter of child-rearing yet. Neither my husband nor I was aligned with a church at the time, although we both had gone as children, albeit to very different ones. Our parents had done their bit; now it was time to do ours.[4]

I'm shocked that someone in Texas would reach Boy Scout age without being able to recognize Jesus Christ on the cross and know at least the bare minimum of the greatest story ever told. Yet that's the world we live in today. Even more disturbing to me was the apparent casual attitude with which this mother approached the need for some "religious education"—determining to get around to it when she could, as though it were one more thing to check off on the list of parental to-dos.

Our first duty as Christ followers is to know the story. In the New Testament, Peter admonished believers to "always be ready to give a defense to anyone who asks you for a reason for the hope that is in you" (1 Pet. 3:15b). Moreover, rather than only knowing the facts of the story, we also must decide if we believe the story. Or are we simply acting out everyone else's interpretation of truth? We can only give a reason for our hope if our lives portray something different because of our role in the story.

A Story to *Believe*

So what is this greatest story ever told, anyway?

A great king appears from a mysterious past to expand His kingdom and to share His vision for a free world where citizens willingly share His life and values. When members of the new world rebel against Him, the king shows His patience. Instead of forcibly restoring order, He begins a long process of developing a relationship with those who are willing to trust Him.

The king's heart is seen most clearly when He disguises Himself as a servant, and, at great personal cost, goes to the rescue of those who have fallen under the control of an evil rebel leader. Although the king secures the ultimate safety and happiness of His citizens, the battle for their hearts and minds goes on. Until He returns, the realm of His kingdom exists in the hearts of all who acknowledge Him as king and trust His offer of forgiveness and everlasting life. The king's story is a story of love and mercy.[5]

That's one way to describe the basic plot of the Bible and what Christ has done for us. People sometimes use the "Roman road" as a tool for a response to this story, using key verses from Paul's letter to the Romans to explain how to become a Christ follower—to live out a belief in the story.

- Romans 3:23: "For all have sinned and fall short of the glory of God." We must all realize that we are sinners—we have gone our way and not God's way, and each of us needs God's forgiveness.

- Romans 5:8: "But God proves His own love for us in that while we were still sinners Christ died for us!" Before we even took a step toward Him, God provided a way to be rescued from our sins, demonstrating His love by giving us the potential for life through the death of His Son, Jesus Christ.

- Romans 6:23: "For the wages of sin is death, but the gift of God is eternal life in Christ Jesus our Lord." If we choose to live apart from God, we will die. However, if we receive Jesus as our Lord and Savior and repent of our sins, we will have eternal life.

- Romans 10:9: "If you confess with your mouth, 'Jesus is Lord,' and believe in your heart that God raised Him from the dead, you will be saved." This is what each person needs to do to move from "religion" to a relationship and become a Christ follower.

- Romans 11:36: "For from Him and through Him and to Him are all things. To Him be the glory forever. Amen." Make a choice for Christ to be your Savior and Lord—the center of your life story because He is your Creator and Sustainer.

It's important to know what you believe in life; otherwise you can't fully embrace your unique role. If you want to be part of an epic that started with the beginning of the world and goes on to eternity, then jump into God's story. Jesus's closest friend, John, described it this way: "In the beginning was the Word, and the Word was with God, and the Word was God. He was with God in the beginning. All things were created through Him, and apart from Him not one thing was created that has been created. Life was in Him, and that life was the light of men. That light shines in the darkness, yet the darkness did not overcome it" (John 1:1–5).

Can you already tell this is the beginning of something that will reveal to us the most profound mysteries of life? This story is simply about God, the glory of His character, the nature of His life, and His desire to share that life with His creatures. It is about God living among us and the mixed response He received to His offer of divine life. "The true light, who gives light to everyone, was coming into the world. He was in the world, and the world was created through Him, yet the world did not recognize Him. He came to His own, and His own people did not receive Him. But to all who did receive Him, He gave them the right to be children of God" (John 1:9–12a).

Perhaps the best part of John's prologue is what I call my favorite Christmas verse: "The Word became flesh and took up residence among us. We observed His glory, the glory as the One and Only Son from the Father, full of grace and truth" (John 1:14). I love the way the *Message* paraphrases this: "The Word became flesh and blood, and moved into the neighborhood. We saw the glory with our own eyes, the one-of-a-kind glory, like Father, like Son, Generous inside and out, true from start to finish." *Immanuel* means "God with us," and that's the crux of our story. He came. He actually *moved into our neighborhood*. He didn't look down from on high, view all our struggling and searching for significance, and choose to shout down words of encouragement: "You can do it! Hang in there!" No, He came. Himself. That's what makes the Christian story different from all other religions.

John Eldredge, in his book *Epic*, pointed out the characteristics of every truly important story:

Notice how all the great stories pretty much follow the same story line. Things were once good, then something awful happened, and now a great battle must be fought or a journey taken. At just the right moment (which feels like the last possible moment), a hero comes and sets things right, and life is found again. It's true of every fairy tale, every myth, every Western, every epic—just about every story you can think of, one way or another. *Braveheart, Titanic, Star Wars, Gladiator, Lord of the Rings*. Why do all these stories follow a similar structure, an archetype, so to speak? Because all of these stories borrow from the Story. From Reality. We hear echoes of it through our lives. Some secret written on our hearts. An adventure, something that requires everything we have, something to be shared with those we love and need. There is a story we just can't seem to escape—a story written on the human heart.[6]

Is your heart longing for more in life? If you're tired of starring in your own small story, that's because God created you to live in the middle of an epic story—one that will have eternal ramifications. Believe it.

A Story to *Live*

But it's not enough to only know the story and believe it. At some point each of us must make a deliberate choice to *live* the story. Are we going to embrace life with abandon, or are we going to continue with same old same old? Consider first, before you make that choice. This story is definitely not a fairy tale; and while there is a "happily ever after" of sorts (eternal life for all who believe), there is also darkness, danger, and distraction ahead. What makes it all worth it is that it is *true*. There is also delight, devotion, and deliverance.

The greatest story ever told is real. It's authentic and truer than we can imagine. Dale Tolmasoff, in his children's book

This Is No Fairy Tale, observed, "This story is very different [from traditional fairy tales]. It really happened. . . . If this were a fairy tale, Jesus would have been born in a big castle in a great kingdom. His parents would have been the king and queen, and all the people in the kingdom would have celebrated the birth of the new prince. The truth is Jesus was born to a poor family in a small country. In fact, he wasn't even born in a house, but in a stable where animals are kept. And no one even knew about it except a few shepherds who came to see him."[7]

What a paradox. The King of kings and Lord of lords humbled Himself to become a helpless little baby. Yes, this story is full of paradox: The last will be first; to gain our life we must lose it; in our weakness He is our strength. Everything is in direct opposition to how the world operates today. No wonder we have a problem communicating this incredible story to others!

Author and pastor Frederick Buechner once received a letter inviting him to speak to a group of ministers on the subject of storytelling. As he contemplated his response to their questions, he realized they had asked him *how* to tell a story instead of *what* stories to tell and to *what end*. So he wrote an essay, "The Two Stories," clearly showing how all Christians are called to live in the middle of God's grand story:

The story of Christ is where we all started from, though we've come so far since then that there are times when you'd hardly know it to listen to us and when we hardly know it ourselves. The story of Jesus is full of darkness as well as of light. . . . He was born, the story begins—the barn that needs cleaning, the sagging steps, the dusty face—and there are times when we have to forget all about the angels and shepherds and star of it, I think, and just let the

birth as a birth be wonder enough, which Heaven
help us it is, this wonder of all wonders. Into a world
that has never been famous for taking special care of
the naked and helpless, he was born in the same old
way to the same old end and in all likelihood howled
bloody murder with the rest of us when they got the
breath going in him and he sensed more or less what
he was in for. . . .

And then it happened. . . . He wasn't dead.
Anymore. The worst we know of darkness, any of us,
was split in two like an atom. The explosion shook
history to its roots, shook even us once to our roots
though it's sometimes hard to remember. . . . Because
of this story of Jesus, each of our own stories is in
countless ways different from what it would have
been otherwise, and that is the other story we have
in us to remember and tell. Our own story. . . . Two
stories then—our own story and Jesus' story, and in
the end, perhaps, they are the same story . . . .

We have it in us to be Christs to each other and
maybe in some unimaginable way to God too—that's
what we have to tell finally. And who knows but
that in the end, by God's mercy, the two stories will
converge for good and all, and though we would
never have had the courage or the faith or the wit to
die for him any more than we have ever managed to
live for him very well either, his story will come true
in us at last.[8]

Will God's story come true in you? It will if you choose
to live it today. To discover more of the unique role God is
calling you to assume in this drama. To pray for direction
on where and how He wants you to serve others. To discipline yourself to literally fight for your life, if needed. To be

so assured of His unconditional love that all other influences pale in comparison to your identity as the son or daughter of the King.

If you've ever wanted to be smack dab in the middle of a love story, here's your chance. For truly this is, more than anything, a love story. One that we can join King David in shouting from the mountaintop, "Your love, GOD, is my song, and I'll sing it! I'm forever telling everyone how faithful you are. I'll never quit telling the story of your love" (Ps. 89:1–2a MSG).

Have you told this story to anyone lately? You know, the one about the Creator who greatly loves His creation, but people turn from Him and go their own way. He tries to win them back through prophets, pestilence, and even perilous journeys, but they still rebel. So the only way He can finally get their attention is to take the biggest risk of all—to become like one of them. He gives up everything to join their humanity and to show them love and a better way, culminating in a final dramatic proof of love by suffering the punishment they deserved through His death on a cross and then miraculously coming back to remind them that all who follow Him will live forever!

Talk about an incredible love story!

And the best part of all is that this one can easily be personalized for any loved one. "*For God so loved ____ that he gave his one and only Son, that [if] ____ believes in him ____ shall not perish but ____ [shall] have eternal life'*" (John 3:16 NIV).

Welcome to the adventure of a lifetime! We are made to live in God's story . . . for God's glory . . . with God's joy. It is only within God's story that our stories find their true meaning and destiny. Know it. Believe it. Live it. And then, don't forget to be a storyteller yourself and pass it along to future generations. Tell it!

⟶ My Life Story ⟵

What were some of your earliest views of God?

How has your view changed over the years?

Do you know by heart the greatest story ever told? How would you write God's story (in your own words) for someone who didn't know it? Write it here.

People can argue with you about theology, but it's harder to argue with your personal experience of God in your life. Write how you have experienced the reality of this story in your own life.

When was the last time you told someone a story that had a meaning you were trying to get across? What was the story and whom did you tell? Where were you and what was the response?

When did you last hear a story that spoke to your heart and caused you to make a change in your life? Who told it and when? What part of it touched you the most? Why do you think it caused this result in you?

What is your favorite Bible story and why?

What is your favorite children's story or book and why?

What is your favorite adult story or book and why?

Do you agree with Scotty Smith (in the epigraph to this chapter) that God has only a bit part in your autobiography of self-fulfillment? Why or why not?

What part do you hope God will have in your life story? Is there a step you could take now to ensure that happens?

The Word became flesh and took up residence among us. We observed His glory, the glory as the One and Only Son from the Father, full of grace and truth.

John 1:14

Chapter 2

Auditioning for Your Role

God acts in history and in your and my brief histories
not as a puppeteer who sets the scene and works the strings
but rather as the great director who no matter what role fate
casts us in conveys to us somehow from the wings, if we have
our eyes, ears, hearts open and sometimes even if we don't,
how we can play those roles in a way to enrich and ennoble
and hallow the whole vast drama of things including our
own small but crucial parts in it.
—Frederick Buechner, *Telling Secrets*

As my teenage daughter Maggie checked in for her audition, I glanced around the theater lobby. Young people of all shapes and sizes were busily filling out forms, reviewing sheet music, and putting on dance shoes. But amid the nervous smiles was a tension as each furtively eyed her neighbor, perhaps thinking, *Is she the one who'll be Sandy?* or *I wonder if I stand a chance as Rizzo even though I'm not Italian.*

Everyone wanted a part in the local repertory theater production of *Grease*. Since it would soon be on Broadway, all rights for smaller productions would cease for years. My

Maggie was seventeen and had her heart set on performing in *Grease*. By the time the opportunity arose again she'd probably be past the age range.

Since Maggie is a performer—voice, dance, and drama—this was definitely not the first audition I'd accompanied her to. In fact, we were well versed in the routine: Bring sheet music for two varying Broadway songs—one ballad and one upbeat (praying for a good accompanist)—be prepared with a dramatic monologue or ready for a cold reading, and wear dance clothes with jazz and character shoes for different routines.

My job? Basically to drive the car and sign the parental release form. I was instructed to keep quiet and not be a pushy stage mother. According to her drama coach, on audition days all the mom is allowed to say is, "I love you."

"No final reminders or encouraging 'You can do it!' cheers?" I asked.

"No, Mama," Maggie replied, rolling her eyes.

I can do silence. I promise. I can do it.

While the first group was summoned to the stage, through the walls I heard Maggie belting "There Are Worse Things I Could Do." She sounded strong and clear. We were off to a great start, I thought.

In auditions each person is trying to convince the director she is the perfect one to play the role he is casting. Many hopefuls try out. A few get callbacks, making the first cut and returning for yet another chance to impress and prove their worth. But only one will get the coveted role. And this important decision is in the hands of the director.

Who will make his story come alive? Who will *become* the character? It's a risk. What if the director chooses wrong? Perhaps someone appears to have the talent and physicality for the role but turns out to be unreliable in rehearsals and refuses direction. Or maybe the director should risk casting that newcomer who shows great promise but lacks experience. Will she blossom into the role or break under the pressure?

At the callbacks for *Grease*, my daughter had to make a difficult decision. She could probably play Rizzo (the part she desperately wanted) but only if she didn't miss rehearsals during spring break. This was an obstacle because our family—scattered far and wide for more than two years—had a family reunion scheduled in Washington State during spring break week. The air tickets were purchased, housing was arranged, and yet it would mean no part in *Grease*.

"I can't say I'm not disappointed, Mama. I am. But I have to pull myself out of the running because spending that week with my sister and brothers is more important than any show," she said with a heavy sigh.

I felt for her. I wanted to orchestrate things and make it work. But I also knew that one of the most important lessons in life is that we often have to make a difficult choice between two good things. This time her role as a sister and daughter won over any role in musical theater.

Later that night, commiserating over pizza, Maggie said, "You know, that was one of my first big rejections."

"But you weren't really rejected. I think they would have given you a part if you hadn't had to miss those rehearsals," I said.

"No, it was a rejection, but that's good for me. If I'm going to be in musical theater, I need to be able to accept disappointments."

She was right. After all, she had been cast as the female lead in the past three musicals she had auditioned for. Both of us knew that was not typical. Life would be full of auditions. But actual *roles*? Well, there's no predicting that.

In the great drama of life, what is the role you have been cast in? When did you audition for it? Whatever made the Director believe you had what it took to pull this off?

I can almost hear you saying, "I never wanted this role, and I certainly didn't try out for it! Life just sort of happened and . . . here I am! I don't even know what my next lines are!"

Well, you're not alone. At some time most of us wonder whatever happened to that fairy-tale life we were supposed to live—you know, the one we dreamed of when we were little girls, all too impatient to grow up and get on with it! Often as I speak to groups of several hundred women, I'll ask them something like, "Has anyone here ever thought, *This is not the life I signed up for! It looks nothing like the life I planned and dreamed and envisioned for myself!?*" As nervous laughter propels hundreds of hands in the air, I turn to them and say very quietly:

"God—the Creator and Sustainer of the universe. God— the One who spun the stars into space and knows the number of hairs on your head. God—the Lover of your soul. That very God has a better plan. Can you trust His choices?"

"What no eye has seen and no ear has heard, and what has never come into a man's heart, is what God has prepared for those who love Him" (1 Cor. 2:9b).

The Director Enlists

God, the Author and Finisher of our faith, is the good Director who casts you in the role of a lifetime. And it is an entirely unique role, as Henri Nouwen confirmed in *The Life of the Beloved*: "Your life and my life are, each of them, one of a kind. No one has ever lived your life or my life before, and no one will live them again. Our lives are unique stones in the mosaic of human existence—priceless and irreplaceable."

If you are a follower of Jesus Christ, then you are a son or daughter of the King of kings. And, if the child of a king, then a prince or princess! "For you are all sons [daughters] of God through faith in Christ Jesus" (Gal. 3:26). "And because you are sons [daughters], God has sent the Spirit of His Son into our hearts, crying, '*Abba*, Father!' So you are no longer a slave, but a son [daughter]; and if a son [daughter], then an heir through God" (Gal. 4:6–7). The apostle Paul wrote those words to emphasize the new relationship. Precisely as an adopted child under Roman law had all legal rights to the father's property, all Christ followers are now sons and daughters and thus heirs, having been adopted into God's family.

It wasn't until I stood in front of a judge in a Seattle courtroom to adopt three children of my own that I came to fully appreciate my own role as an adopted daughter of the King. "The Spirit Himself testifies together with our spirit that we are God's children, and if children, also heirs—heirs of God and co-heirs with Christ" (Rom. 8:16–17a). What an amazing concept! And what a pivotal part of my own identity and life story.

Even though I don't possess great material wealth, all I have is fully available to my (now four) children. Because of my great love for them, I willingly give of my resources, my strength, my creativity, my wisdom, my encouragement, and my possessions each day. Once they were not my children, but now they are. How sad I would be if they acted as though I'd never come along! How useless I'd feel if they never came to me for all the blessings I so desire to give them. But if I feel this way, how much more so must my heavenly Father feel when I run around acting like an orphan and not as His chosen child!

As one lawyer pointed out, "To be adopted ultimately depends upon the choice of someone else. Only parents can petition to adopt a child, not vice versa. Paul says that God chooses us to be His children. He also says that the motivating force behind this choice is love."[1] Only the Director can cast you in your role. He calls and enlists you to come on board. "Look at how great a love the Father has given us, that we should be called God's children. And we are!" (1 John 3:1a).

Do you know that you are a princess? Mia Thermopolis doesn't know she's a princess, that her father was a king. In *The Princess Diaries* movie, Mia (played by Anne Hathaway) is an awkward fifteen-year-old girl who wears glasses and has a crush on the high school hunk. As a girl who so much can't stand being the center of attention that she throws up during debate class, she's stunned and horrified when her coolly continental grandmother (Julie Andrews) shows up and informs her that she's the crown princess of the European principality Genovia. After Mia undergoes "princess lessons" and an extreme makeover from her queenly grandmother, she blossoms into a confident, radiant girl—despite the worries and pressure that her newfound status brings.[2]

But knowing we are adopted princesses and living like it are two different things. It takes awhile sometimes to learn to trust and love our heavenly Father. The story is told of a wealthy man back in the nineteenth century who adopted about six street orphans and moved them into his mansion, promising to provide for them as his own sons. But every night they cried themselves to sleep. You see, nothing in their lives had prepared them to trust that what this man, their new father, told them was true. Yes, they had food and clothes that day, but what about the next? These newly adopted children lived in fear until the man's wife had an idea. What if the man and his wife put a small loaf of bread under each child's pillow each night so the children could feel secure in knowing there would be food the next day?

And it worked. Holding on to the bread, they no longer cried and feared waking up in need. And more importantly, as they came to know their father and felt secure in his love, they no longer even needed the bread to remind them of his provision. Isn't that how it is with us too? The better we know our heavenly Father, the easier it is to trust Him in every way.

My friend Andrea Stephens reaches out to young women through her B.A.B.E. Seminars, telling them they are Beautiful, Accepted, Blessed, and Eternally significant. Each week in my home I teach my own group of teen Girlz4God, and we grapple with how to live their roles as godly teenagers in the middle of secular high school society. It includes studying the script (Bible), taking cues from the Director (God), and, most importantly, playing to an audience of One.

This is where it gets tricky. Once we've been cast in a unique role, we want to savor rave reviews from everyone. And we find ourselves doing some version of the wicked queen's daily litany: "Mirror, mirror, on the wall, who's the fairest of them all?" Inevitably she heard only, "Snow White is fairer by far." There was always someone else. What does this have to do with twenty-first-century women? Surely none of us are like that; in fact, some of us try to avoid mirrors altogether, certainly not bask in front of them, right?

While this may be true, I regret to admit I have acted like the wicked queen too often, seeking external validation for who I am, how I look, and what I do. Think about it. Every time we turn to others to give us meaning or worth, it's like consulting the magic mirror. Only more and more we get a response that it is someone *else* who is the fairest or smartest or richest of all. There's always someone else. We can never keep up, much less excel. What to do?

Change the audience. All of us have specific people we hope to please, and they have potential to either elevate us to the heights or send us plummeting to the depths, but only if we let them. We need to take away the power of those negative folk. Oh yes, they will still be in the auditorium of our lives, but we can require them to take the seats way in the back.

Andrea Stephens encourages teens to let God be their Director and primary audience:

His glow gives off warmth that reaches out and draws you in. His presence calms your heart. His love fills your empty places. His acceptance heals the brokenness. His peace replaces your fears. His gentleness lifts your inadequacies. His strength rushes to strengthen your weaknesses. His joy overtakes your sadness. In His presence you feel so different, yet so natural, so calm, so secure, so safe, so genuine. So you! Meet your new audience. Your audience of One! And He doesn't critique you based on your performance, abilities or achievements. No, His applause is rooted in His love for you and in His joy at being your heavenly Father. With God as your audience, His acceptance of you is both unconditional and complete. Unconditional. No strings attached. Without limits. Complete. Lacking nothing. Full. Maximized. Without reservation. Think about that.[3]

In William Shakespeare's *As You Like It*, Jaques says, "All the world's a stage, And all the men and women merely players: They have their exits and their entrances; And one man in his time plays many parts." Author and speaker Jan Coleman elaborated: "If we believe in a sovereign God who directs the affairs of men, then we can't help but see ourselves, created and designed by Him, with a written-for-us part to play in His grand story, in His perfect time."[4]

So, believe in God's sovereignty and don't let anyone else define who you are. God is the One who defines you, and to Him, you are His beloved!

The Director Equips

Perhaps you've been cast in a role and you feel totally inadequate to play the part. I know this has been true in nearly every major assignment God has given me in life, especially when I became a wife and mother all in the same year. Talk about a major learning curve! Not only, like Prissy in *Gone with the Wind*, did I "know nothin' 'bout birthin' babies," but I didn't know what to do as they grew up either! Yet with every parental encounter these past twenty-three years, I have turned with hope to the promise found in 1 Thessalonians 5:24: "He who calls you is faithful, who also will do it." When you are enlisted, you are also equipped. With God, it's a package deal. Nothing in your life is wasted; it's all used to prepare you for the role you're called to play.

I think fondly of a scene from the movie *Simon Birch*, in which two young boys are at the local swimming hole, practicing holding their breath under water. They are determined to do it longer and longer each time. What is significant is that these two boys, growing up in 1964, are both misfits in their small Maine town—Joe is illegitimate and Simon is small (born with Morquio's syndrome, a type of dwarfism). While they both have many misadventures and withstand the brunt of cruel jokes, Simon doesn't lose heart because he truly believes God has made him the way he is for a special, heroic purpose. This is what keeps him going, even when one of his actions inadvertently causes the death of someone he loves.

The viewer perhaps sees this as a crutch: "Well, if that's what helps this little boy keep going, then it's all fine and good." But the truth in this particular life story is that Simon is uniquely equipped for a life-and-death heroic role that calls for someone tiny who can hold his breath under water a long time. When that need arises, he is enlisted, equipped, and empowered to live out his story with courage, faithfulness, and, yes, ultimately sacrifice. Years later his friend Joe, now grown up with his own son Simon in tow, kneels at Simon Birch's grave and reflects on how knowing him changed the course of his life—for good.[5]

An important part of my life story has been the fact that my eldest son, Justin, was born with mental retardation. Today he is a responsible young man who lives in an apartment, has worked at Red Lobster for ten years, and excels in Special Olympics. Sometimes it's hard to admit that, yes, developmental disabilities do "flavor" the family unit—with both occasional frustration and frequent inspiration. I confess that in the early years of teaching him, I was often impatient and perplexed with the constant repetition needed for him to learn simple tasks. And yet, God clearly reminded me of my early twenties when I was a teacher for the blind. Every day then was spent celebrating hard-fought small victories for my clients. Surely those experiences were like an investment in the bank account of my life—one I would eventually draw on when faced with this new calling of raising a son with special needs. Nothing in our lives is wasted!

Do you know how you are uniquely equipped for the life you are called to lead today? Perhaps it's time to reflect on such things so that you don't turn around one day and discover you have missed your calling. One of my favorite authors, Max Lucado, gave this perspective in *Cure for the Common Life*: "God has designed you and gifted you in a unique way so you can fulfill the special purpose He has in mind for you. As you increasingly understand your giftedness, you can build your life, work and your ministry on God's unique will for you. Use your uniqueness (what you do) to make a big deal out of God (why you do it) every day of your life (where you do it)."[6]

He offered a simple formula called S.T.O.R.Y. in order to examine . . .

- *Strengths*: What verbs do you use to describe how you get things done?
- *Topics*: What nouns describe what you get completely absorbed in working with?
- *Optimal conditions*: What triggers you with the best setting to get you motivated?
- *Relationships*: What kind of role with others do you seek in the task?
- *Yes!*: What are you doing when you achieve this joyous affirmation and fulfillment?

Lucado encouraged us to prayerfully discern when all these elements converge. He called that our sweet spot and said that only then are we truly living out our life story.[7]

I agree with Max. Occasionally people will lament that they wish they could be young again, and I reply, "I don't want to be young again. I just wish I could have known myself better when I was young." We attack life with such fits and starts and try on different personas like so many shoes, hoping one will be the perfect fit. But it takes time and experience—both successes and failures—to finally discover and reveal our sweet spot. For too many of us that happens later in life. For me, it has been a journey of discovery, and even with the slight regret mentioned earlier, I also see God's hand on me during my youth when He was guiding and confirming gifts and calling in the areas of communication and compassion.

In my hand right now is a thirty-three-year-old piece of paper—my senior student résumé from the Furman University placement office. Daddy sent it to me recently when he was going through files. As I peruse this, I realize that much has changed. And yet, I'm also amazed at the pattern revealed, even back then. The job I was looking for was something in the field of "public relations, communications, journalism, social services." And my hobbies were "reading, writing, music, theater, art, photography, films, pottery, mountain climbing, and crafts." Well, I haven't done a lot of mountain climbing in the past twenty-five years, but the rest still fits! And the first job I got with this résumé was as a writer for a small magazine, *Carolina Country*. And I'm still writing!

God has chosen us and created us with special gifting to serve in a place of His choosing. And we are never quite content until we arrive at that place. Os Guinness pointed this out in *The Call*: "Somehow we humans are never happier than when we are expressing the deepest gifts that are truly us."

"It's in Christ that we find out who we are and what we are living for. Long before we first heard of Christ and got our hopes up, he had his eye on us, had designs on us for glorious living, part of the overall purpose he is working out in everything and everyone" (Eph. 1:11–12 MSG).

The Director Empowers

God enlists each of His followers to participate in what He is doing to bring about His kingdom here on earth. But He not only calls us; He also promises to equip and empower us for the daunting task ahead. Perhaps one of the greatest legacies of C. S. Lewis was that in his *Chronicles of Narnia* he actually empowered children to believe they were important players in the greatest story ever told. Andrew Adamson, director of the film *The Lion, the Witch and the Wardrobe*, pointed out this effect on children: "They go from being in this world where they're treated as children—they're being pushed around and disenfranchised and fragmented as a family by World War II. And they go to a land where they are no longer referred to as children; they're kings and queens, and they are ultimately the thing that's going to save this land. They go from being children to warriors and that's such an empowering story for children."[8]

Anyone who has seen that movie can't help but remember the scene in which Peter, Susan, Edmund, and Lucy all don the clothing for battle—each armed with exactly what he or she needs. They are ready to take on heroic responsibilities not because they feel worthy, but because Aslan himself promises to be with them and empower them for the huge task at hand.[9] To this day I have a silver charm on my key chain that says "Future Queen" to remind me of this empowering story in Narnia.

When Mike and I were expecting our fourth child, we prayed about the name and decided if we had a girl, we would name her after the queen of Scotland in the twelfth century. In our book of saints we had discovered that Queen Margaret was a godly wife and mother and did much to help the poor. She also is credited for bringing Christianity to the throne when she married King Malcolm. In fact, the oldest edifice still standing at Edinburgh Castle is Margaret's Chapel, built by her son, King David, in 1200 to honor his mother. Our Maggie has always known she was named for a queen and thinks it's pretty special, especially when she visited Margaret's Chapel.

There was another queen empowered to do far more than she had imagined in a role she never expected. I love the story of Esther, found in the Old Testament. Here we have a Jewish orphan girl living in exile in Persia with her cousin

Mordecai. "Mordecai had a cousin named Hadassah, whom he had brought up because she had neither father nor mother. This girl, who was also known as Esther, was lovely in form and features, and Mordecai had taken her as his own daughter when her father and mother died" (Esther 2:7 NIV). Yes, she was a beauty and thus captured the attention of King Xerxes conducting auditions for a new queen. "Now the king was attracted to Esther more than to any of the other women, and she won his favor and approval more than any of the other virgins. So he set a royal crown on her head and made her queen instead of Vashti. And the king gave a great banquet, Esther's banquet, for all his nobles and officials. He proclaimed a holiday throughout the provinces and distributed gifts with royal liberality" (Esther 2:17–18 NIV). But you don't have to read far to discover that Esther was far more than merely a looker. She had depth and a deep faith that God was with her, even in this new script not of her choosing.

Recently during winter break, I had my Girlz4God teens over for movie night, and we watched the film version of Esther's life *One Night with the King*.[10] The great thing was that I was able to pause the DVD and explain things ("What is a eunuch?" "Eeeew gross!") as well as point out specific biblical references and verses we had studied. But a challenge was helping them understand the whole idea of maintaining palace protocol, such as a queen forbidden to enter the presence of the king unless she was summoned. The penalty? Death. That seemed quite foreign to these independent-minded young women of the twenty-first century, and yet it is integral to understanding the great risk Esther took as she dared to live out the life story God gave her.

When Esther became queen of Persia, she did not tell Xerxes of her Jewish heritage. Her people were in exile and were also in danger of annihilation because of the vengeance of Haman, Xerxes' right-hand man, who had it in for Mordecai and his people. "When Haman saw that Mordecai would not kneel down or pay him honor, he was enraged. Yet having learned who Mordecai's people were, he scorned the idea of killing only Mordecai. Instead Haman looked for a way to destroy all Mordecai's people, the Jews, throughout the whole kingdom of Xerxes" (3:5–6 NIV). Now was the time for Esther to act and fulfill the major role God prepared for her. She had already had a whole year of spa treatments. She had already been chosen over all the other harem women to be queen. She had won the respect of Hegai, the head eunuch, and of her attendants in the palace. And she had the love of her husband, the king. But now she dared to live out a story that placed her directly in opposition to palace protocol.

Mordecai pleaded with her to intervene on behalf of the Jewish people and save them from the attacks Haman had planned. "Do not think that because you are in the king's house you alone of all the Jews will escape. For if you remain silent at this time, relief and deliverance for the Jews will arise from another place, but you and your father's family will perish. And who knows but that you have come to royal position for such a time as this?" (4:13–14 NIV).

Esther's immediate response was to ask the Jews to fast and pray with her: "Do not eat or drink for three days, night or day. I and my maids will fast as you do. When this is done, I will go to the king, even though it is against the law. And if I perish, I perish" (4:16b NIV).

God answered Esther's prayers and not only gave her courage and strength to face her king but also gave her his favor when she entered his presence unbidden. She used her audience with the king to reveal Haman's true plan to hang Mordecai and attack the Jews, then she entreated Xerxes to save her people with a royal edict, sealed by his signet ring. He not only gave her what she asked, but he punished Haman's deceit by death and elevated Mordecai to rule his household.

God's people were saved, and to this day the Jews celebrate Esther's role through the annual feast of Purim. "For the Jews it was a time of happiness and joy, gladness and honor. In every province and in every city, wherever the edict of the king went, there was joy and gladness among the Jews, with feasting and celebrating" (8:16–17a NIV).

You don't have to know all the dimensions of your role in God's story right here and right now. But you can discover more each day exactly whom He is calling you to be for His kingdom "for such a time as this."

— My Life Story —

As soon as I finish this book, I have only two weeks left to finish another important book—a scrapbook for my youngest daughter's eighteenth birthday. I'm centering it on one important theme in Maggie's life—her first eighteen years of performances. Included are dozens of pictures, playbills, tickets, clippings, stickers, and stories of her growing up into acting, singing, and dancing.

But here's the really amazing part—she has been doing these things *from an early age!* There are pictures of her using a large wooden spoon for a microphone at age two and singing on the "stage" (our fireplace hearth in the center of the living room). From her earliest days, this theme has been a passion and a gift—one that Maggie has offered back to the Lord to use as He will.

What are some of the themes that thread their way throughout your life? Gardening, grace, recovery, romance—use your imagination!

Take one of those themes and put together a small scrapbook (materials can be purchased at any craft store) of how this theme is part of your life. Include photos, cards, journaling, and stickers that help to show why this has been important to you. Afterward, share what you discovered about yourself in the process.

At what point in your life story did you feel the least adequate for the role God called you to?

Recall how:
- The Director enlisted you.

- The Director equipped you.

- The Director empowered you.

Use Max Lucado's acrostic S.T.O.R.Y. to discover your own sweet spot:

- *Strengths*: What verbs describe how you get things done?

- *Topics*: What nouns describe the tasks that completely absorb you?

- *Optimal conditions*: What is the best setting to motivate you?

- *Relationships*: What kind of role with others do you seek in the task?

- *Yes!*: What are you doing when you achieve this joyous affirmation and fulfillment?

What no eye has seen and no ear has heard,
and what has never come into a man's heart,
is what God has prepared for those who love Him.
I Corinthians 2:9

Chapter 3

Studying Your Script

At any age, if we are to face life with integrity and purpose,
we must know that our lives do mean something, that we
matter to someone, and that whatever story we have lived,
it has brought us to this point. . . . Remembering our story
helps us journey into wholeness. In the process of remembering
and sharing our stories, we restore those parts of ourselves
we have forgotten, suppressed or denied. . . .
As we touch the stories of Christ and connect them
with our stories, we find wholeness.
—Richard L. Morgan, *Remembering Your Story*

I clutch the boarding pass as I enter the Edwardian splendor
that is the *Titanic*. My script says that I am fifty-year-old
Helene Baxter from Montreal and that I'm traveling with my
adult daughter and son. It is April 10, 1912, and I'm sailing
home on the *Titanic* after seeking medical advice in Europe
for my heart condition. I'm a first-class passenger and my
stateroom is B58. Will I survive the ordeal ahead? Will my
children? How does the script of my life play out in the real-
life drama ahead?

Of course, I am not actually the real Helene and this is
not the real *Titanic*, but ninety-five years (to the day) after

the fateful sinking, my family and I are exploring the "Titanic Artifact Exhibition" at the Royal British Columbia Museum in Victoria, Canada. Like all visitors, the six of us have been given scripts about real *Titanic* passengers. Each of us studies his role as we pass through galleries that authentically recreate first- and third-class corridors, cabins, and even the outdoor café. Immersed in the passenger experience, we are amazed at the opulence and excess that was this "unsinkable" ship.

Mingling among us in character is *Titanic*'s Captain Edward Smith—White Star Line's most prized captain—who eventually went down with his ship. Also along to chat with us is Margaret Tobin Brown, the American socialite, philanthropist, and activist. Better known as "the unsinkable Molly Brown," she commandeered a lifeboat during the actual sinking and urged the women to row when the men gave out. What makes the experience all the more realistic is that these actors present stories taken from transcripts of firsthand accounts to bring to life the forebodings, experiences, and contradictory opinions of the *Titanic* disaster. All around us are 281 artifacts recovered from the shipwreck site thirty-eight hundred meters below the surface of the North Atlantic Ocean—crew jackets, perfume bottles, fancy china, and shoes.

Perhaps the most haunting exhibit hall is the one that's almost completely dark, except for vivid stars and a huge iceberg (literally made of ice and begging to be touched), and gives the grim statistics of more than fifteen hundred lives lost in the icy sea that night, most from hypothermia, not drowning. We are silent passing through the various displays, and I can't help but wonder how Helene must have felt in all the chaos and confusion of that crisis. At the end of the exhibit are the lists of who survived and perished. Helene and her daughter lived, but her son died. In fact, of all the scripts our family was given, all three women (my daughters and I) lived and all three men (my husband and sons) died. It's a sobering thought as we move back to the future.

Upon reflection, what we are experiencing this day in April is more than merely observing history, it is—even if for a brief moment—an opportunity to step into someone else's shoes and vicariously live a pivotal event in that person's life. Museum director Pauline Rafferty says the exhibit isn't only about the sinking of the *Titanic:* "It reflects the impact this historic event continues to have on all of us almost a century later. And it tells the stories and honors the memories of the people who lived through—and lost their lives during—this tragic incident."[1]

Do you sometimes wonder about your own life script? What would a boarding-pass-sized synopsis of your life reveal? I often beg God to show me the script so that I can play it out in the best way possible. But that is not how God allows us to live our lives. He gives us what we need to know each moment of each day as it comes, and we must, in turn, make choices that can change the whole course of our lives.

While we can't predict the future, we can review the past. God said in Deuteronomy 32:7, "Remember the days of old; consider the years long past. Ask your father, and he will tell you, your elders, and they will teach you." What does the script so far tell us about our lives? In my season of middle age, I have found great value in remembering themes and incidents from my own life that help me to better understand who I am and how I can live forward in a more vital way.

Counselor and author Dr. Dan Allender agrees that while everyone's life is a story, "most people don't know how to read their life in a way that reveals their story. They miss the deeper meaning in their life, and they have little sense of how God has written their story to reveal himself and his own story." That's why we must do the hard work of studying our script—thinking back through our lives, discovering who we are, and pinpointing our evolving role in God's drama. "Our story is truer than any other reality we know, and each of us must discover the meaning of what God has written as our life story. In our story God shows us what he's up to and what he wants us to be about."[2]

Don't you want to know what God is up to in your life? Sören Kierkegaard once said, "Life can only be understood backwards, but it must be lived forwards." In a writer's workbook I read, "Our stories give our lives structure and meaning. The word *story* shares the same root as *history*. Both root us to a time and place and heritage. But our stories are not, strictly speaking, history. They are our history as we remember it. They are facts, impressions, and emotions, all filtered through the rest of our life stories."[3]

Different people look at the same life and often see disparate stories. My life as I remember it and even as I live it today is filtered through my emotions and other experiences. Have you ever read about yourself in a magazine or newspaper? Sometimes, depending on which quotes are used and how they are placed, you may even wonder if it's really you! Recently a local newspaper journalist interviewed me for a feature story on my writing and speaking. We covered so much territory that I can't wait to see what thread she will use to pull it together.

Later she e-mailed interesting follow-up questions: "What do the women in your audiences ask? What do they want to know?" I felt like responding, "How much time do you have?" Since I speak both in this country and elsewhere, the people in my audiences represent a vast variety of questions and concerns. But those that inevitably come up include "How can I know what God wants me to do and be?" and "Does my life really make a difference?" No matter what our age or stage in life, we all want to make sure that we matter—that the world is somehow better because we lived.

When you intentionally take time to remember your life, you will discover that it indeed has meaning. Your story matters, and you alone can fulfill the significant role God has for you in the larger story of His kingdom. One way to pursue that reality is to do what our Jewish brothers and sisters have done in the past—offer stones of remembrance.

Many of us have short memories. We forget and make the same mistakes over and over again. Recently I called my younger sister to ask her to remember *for* me something from our childhood. "I'm having a hard time getting the facts straight. Will you remind me again what it was like?" So she nailed it.

God's chosen people seem to have had memory problems too. The Old Testament Hebrew word for "remembering one" is *zakar*. My personal favorite story of remembrance is found in Joshua. You may recall that the Israelites wandered in the desert for forty years. They could have crossed over to the Promised Land much earlier, but they chose to fear the enemy instead of believe in God's great power. After spying out the land, Joshua and Caleb had urged them to go forward, but they were outnumbered by other spies who predicted doom. Now it was forty long years later, and Moses had died, leaving Joshua in charge. Once again the Israelites were up against powerful foes—the Canaanites, Hittites, Hivites, Perizzites, Girgashites, Amorites, and Jebusites.

But Joshua knew that God was with him and had promised the people, "Consecrate yourselves, because the Lord will do wonders among you tomorrow" (Josh. 3:5b). And He did. At God's command the priests carried the ark of the covenant and placed their feet into the middle of an overflowing Jordan River. The entire time they stood there, the waters were held back, allowing more than forty thousand Israelites to cross safely into Canaan. "The priests carrying the ark of the LORD's covenant stood firmly on dry ground in the middle of the Jordan, while all Israel crossed on dry ground until the entire nation had finished crossing the Jordan" (3:17).

Indeed God was with them and further commanded them to establish stones of remembrance to commemorate His faithfulness in bringing them into the Promised Land. "Then Joshua set up in Gilgal the 12 stones they had taken from the Jordan, and he said to the Israelites, 'When your children ask their fathers in the future, "What is the meaning of these stones?" you should tell your children, "Israel crossed the Jordan on dry ground." For the LORD your God dried up the waters of the Jordan before you until you had crossed over, just as the LORD your God did to the Red Sea, which He dried up before us until we had crossed over. This is so that all the people of the earth may know that the LORD's hand is mighty, and so that you may always fear the LORD your God'" (4:20–24).

Begin studying your life script and placing your own stones of remembrance along the way so that you, too, will be prompted to pass along stories of God's faithfulness. Here are exercises that have helped me in this process.

Seasonal Stones

In his midlife journal known as the book of Ecclesiastes, King Solomon mused about the seasons of life: "There is an occasion for everything, and a time for every activity under heaven: a time to give birth and a time to die; a time to plant and a time to uproot; a time to kill and a time to heal; a time to tear down and a time to build; a time to weep and a time to laugh; a time to mourn and a time to dance; a time to throw stones and a time to gather stones; a time to embrace and a time to avoid embracing; a time to search and a time to count as lost; a time to keep and a time to throw away; a time to tear and a time to sew; a time to be silent and a time to speak; a time to love and a time to hate; a time for war and a time for peace. . . . He has made everything appropriate in its time" (3:1–8, 11a).

Each time of life has its own peculiar perks and disadvantages. Remember when you proudly stated your age using "and a half"? Remember when you couldn't wait to grow up and be sixteen so you could drive? Remember the first day your baby went to school all day and you immediately took a loooong shower? Because you could! Or, if you're old enough, remember the first time you availed yourself of the senior discount, comfortable enough in your own skin to think, *This isn't so bad after all.*

Why not take time to think back on the various seasons of your life thus far and pull out your own stones of remembrance? Spiritual autobiographer Richard L. Morgan offers a "Seasons of Life" calendar in which each month represents seven years of life.[4] (See pp. 50–51.)

It was a bit daunting to circle the month of my life right now. According to this chart, I am currently in August, and December is just around the corner. How sobering is that! What can this kind of exercise do? Well, first, it helps us to face the reality of life and to decide to move forward with greater purpose. We have no time to waste!

But, second, we can place next to each season of life a stone of remembrance—a milestone from that time of childhood, teen years, or midlife. Think through the stories from your life and write down at least one that represents who you were and what God was doing in you at that time. And if you can't remember, ask someone else who was there.

It's not hard to determine my own seasonal stone from the April season of life (ages twenty-two to twenty-eight). In December 1976, at age twenty-three, I was the chaperone for a busload of college students going from Montreat, North Carolina, to the Urbana '76 Missions Convention in Illinois. During that week God clearly called me to deepen my commitment to Him and offer myself to go anywhere and do anything He asked of me. It was, quite literally, a turning point in my life, and I have never looked back.

Within six months I had left my job as a teacher for the blind with the state of North Carolina and enrolled at Gordon-Conwell Theological Seminary in Boston. The figurative stone came on the day I met my new faculty adviser, Dr. J. Christy Wilson Jr. He had prechosen a verse for me to claim, and when he spoke these words into my heart, I knew the power of the Holy Spirit in a fresh way: "I will lead the blind by a way they did not know; I will guide them on paths they have not known. I will turn darkness to light in front of them, and rough places into level ground. This is what I will do for them, and I will not forsake them" (Isa. 42:16). Tears come to my eyes as I vividly remember Dr. Wilson offering me that promise thirty years ago. And God has not forsaken me.

Significant Stones

Another way to review your life is to remember significant events. Richard Morgan suggests making a "life map" noting the places you have lived. Put a large A (alpha) to the far left of a sheet of paper and write your birth year and birthplace. To the far right of the paper put a large *T* (for today) and write this year and where you currently live. Fill in the line with locations and dates. Below the line, write out significant stones of remembrance in those places. You can call those *Turning Points*. This will give you a fresh view of your life story.[5]

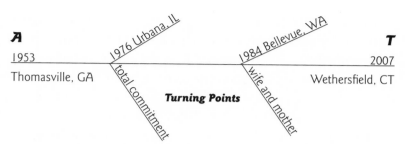

Samuel, an Old Testament prophet, priest, and judge over Israel, also placed a stone of remembrance and called it Ebenezer, which means "stone of help." In his lifetime there had been twenty years of sorrow in Israel (because of disobedience and idol worship), and Samuel had boldly told the people that if they were truly sorry, they should do something about it and get rid of all their idols: "If you are returning to the LORD with all your heart, get rid of the foreign gods and the Ashtoreths that are among you, dedicate yourselves to the LORD, and worship only Him. Then He will rescue you from the hand of the Philistines" (1 Sam. 7:3).

So the people gathered at Mizpah to fight the Philistines. At Samuel's instruction, they poured water on the ground before the Lord as a sign of repentance for sin, turning from idols, and indicating a decision to obey God once more. God ushered them into victory, and as a result of this significant event, "Samuel took a stone and set it upright between Mizpah and Shen. He named it Ebenezer, explaining, 'The LORD has helped us to this point'" (v. 12).

One of my significant stones placed on the life map would be *"1984–Bellevue, Washington."* I was in my early thirties when I got married, adopted three children, moved from San Francisco to the Seattle area, and began a whole new life as an at-home mother, freelance writer, and wife of a college minister. That particular personal Ebenezer marks God's faithfulness in bringing me the desires of my heart—husband and children (finally!). And it marks a time of intense struggle through radical change, a time that brought me to my knees and enabled me to experience God's presence and provision in new ways. It was a significant turning point.

Soul-Shaping Stones

Perhaps the hardest stones of remembrance we have in our life stories are those that reflect times of intense soul shaping—events and circumstances that, though they were difficult at the time, were used of God to grow us spiritually. These are also important to remember as you reflect on your life. Every life is made of both sunshine and shadow times. In my book *Quilts from Heaven*, I talk about the Amish quilt pattern "sunshine and shadow" as a metaphor for celebrations and crises of our lives.[6] This particular quilt contains a row of dark or black squares, followed by a row of beautiful jewel-toned squares, then the dark, then the bright. The entire quilt is a striking contrast between dark and bright colors.

All of us would probably enjoy only celebrations—bright colors in our life stories. But the dark is also necessary for soul shaping. It's part of the perfect pattern God has designed. One exercise to help you remember is to draw a horizontal line on a piece of paper. Above the line, draw circles representing stones of celebration, and below the line draw circles representing stones of crises. Put inside each circle/stone a phrase or two that shares the spiritual growth you experienced as a result of that celebration or crisis.

Jacob was a man who certainly saw both sunshine and shadow in his life. In fact, after he deceived his father, Isaac, and stole his brother Esau's blessing, he had to flee for his life. Finding only a stone for a pillow, he slept in the wilderness and dreamed of a ladder going up to heaven, with angels ascending and descending it. He heard the Lord say, "All the peoples on earth will be blessed through you and your offspring. Look, I am with you and will watch over you wherever you go. I will bring you back to this land, for I will not leave you until I have done what I have promised you" (Gen. 28:14b–15).

Jacob felt he had been given a promise and a second chance! He took his stone pillow and turned it into a stone of remembrance by pouring oil on it and naming it Bethel, which means "house of God." Then he made a pledge to God, saying that because God had blessed him, he would always follow God. This was a soul-shaping time for Jacob, and God did bless him, though there were still crises ahead.

One of my soul-shaping stones commemorates God's work in my brokenness. Our family experienced discouragement and a sense of being uprooted when we moved to New England sixteen years ago. I was overwhelmed with four children ages two to sixteen, and I felt like a failure in marriage, motherhood, and ministry. But my own personal Bethel was that God stooped down and began to work in me a grace tutorial, helping me for the first time in my life to understand and embrace grace—the gift of God we don't deserve and can never earn.[7] My soul-shaping stone is represented by the sign on the door of our parsonage, naming it Gracehaven with the promise "My grace is sufficient for you, for power is perfected in weakness" (2 Cor. 12:9).

God's grace truly has been my sufficiency. God has not forsaken me. And He has certainly led me on countless new and challenging paths. Taking time to remember our lives by studying the script is important but only so far as it helps us to look ahead. When I'm driving, I spend most of my time viewing directional signs and traffic lights in front of me, with only an occasional glance in my rearview mirror to see where I've been. There must be a balance. We are not to live in the past but learn from it—and then move on into more of God's big story.

∽ My Life Story ∽

I have a new T-shirt that says "Rewrite Your Script." If you were to rewrite the script of your own life, what would it look like?

In *Remembering Your Story*, spiritual autobiographer Richard L. Morgan reminded us, "Looking back is not simply reminiscing; it is looking back to become aware of new possibilities. In that way the future becomes a part of our present being, allowing our present circumstances to shape the future before it happens."

In the "Seasons of Life" calendar, each month represents seven years of life. Using the list below, circle which month you are in right now. . . . Then, next to each month write words or phrases representing significant moments at that time of your life.

January / ages 0–7

February / ages 8–14

March / ages 15–21

April / ages 22–28

May / ages 29–35

June / ages 36–42

July / ages 43–49

August / ages 50–56

September / ages 57–63

October / ages 64–70

November / ages 71–77

December / ages 78–X

If you could relive *one day* in your life so far, which day would it be and why? What, if anything, would you have changed about that day and to what end?

What are the most important and frequently told stories when your family gathers? Why do you think this is so? Are these stories true?

Using the exercises we discussed in this chapter, take several large stones and write on them words that represent spiritual turning points in your life. Place them somewhere to help you remember God's faithfulness.

Consecrate yourselves,
because the LORD will do wonders among you tomorrow.
Joshua 3:5

Chapter 4

Heroes

You are a story. You are not merely the possessor and teller of a
number of stories; you are a well-written, intentional story that is
authored by the greatest Writer of all time, and even before time and
after time. The weight of those words, if you believe them even for
brief snippets of time, can change the trajectory of your life.
Dan Allender, *To Be Told*

Are you the hero of your life story?
Every story has a protagonist—the hero, if you will. This
term originates from Greek mythology and folklore in which
heroes represented all that was good and noble in the culture.
The most important characteristic was typically a willingness
to sacrifice self for the greater good. Today other traits come
to mind, such as desire to make a positive difference, willingness to take risks and action, perseverance in the face of dif-
ficulties, ability to learn from failure, and a genuine love for
other people.

Where are the heroes of today? Too often when we look
up to sports figures, those in public service (such as the 9/11
firefighters and rescue workers), clergy, and even well-meaning
parents, we discover flaws that would deem them, according
to the Greek terminology, "tragic heroes." Fame isn't all it's
cracked up to be.

But everyone, it seems, wants to be famous.

A recent poll by the Pew Research Center revealed that for 51 percent of eighteen- to twenty-five-year-olds "being famous" was their generation's second most important life goal ("getting rich" the most important goal, 81 percent). Ironically, "developing a meaningful philosophy of life" dropped in importance from 86 percent in 1967 to 45 percent in 2005.[1]

Maybe I should say that everyone, it seems, wants to be rich and famous.

And it doesn't seem to matter much how you acquire your fame. There is an online Web site that guarantees to help make you famous. Listen to it's lure: "Here at *IWannaBeFamous!*, we feature one ordinary person at a time. Being a famous celebrity is not so bad after all. Sometimes fame and being a celebrity brings big fortune, but other times it brings headaches. Keep in mind that once you're famous you'll need an agent, a photographer, a bodyguard, an accountant, a therapist, a lawyer, and perhaps a good plastic surgeon. Are you up to the challenge of receiving instant fame through the Internet? If so, then send us your photo today and tell us why you wanna be famous!" Needless to say, I didn't click further to check out that week's "famous person."

Then there are those who are famous for being famous. That's actually a documented new twenty-first-century term—*famous for being famous*. (Does the name Paris Hilton immediately come to mind?) It "refers to someone who attains celebrity status for no particular identifiable reason. The individual will often be somehow attached to others who are considered to be famous for another reason. The term is a pejorative, suggesting that the person has no particular talents or abilities. Even when their fame arises from a particular talent or action on their part, the term will sometimes still apply if their fame is disproportionate to what they earned through their own talent or work. A person who is considered famous for being famous will sometimes choose to capitalize on their image for fame and money."[2]

It used to be that people had to actually achieve something or believe something before they were elevated to fame status—back when we had heroes we admired because they deserved our admiration and respect. But now people are even confused about what a hero truly is. When asked, "Who are your heroes?" in an educational survey, one young woman, Naomi, pointed out heroic qualities such as thoughtfulness, responsibility, and great strength of personality: "Mostly a real hero must think about those around him before he thinks of himself. Often they are subject to ridicule but still stand by their beliefs. Maybe a hero doesn't have to do anything for a large mass of people, but for an individual. You can be held just as highly by that one person and be their hero, because heroism is in the eye of the beholder."

While Naomi refused to name her own heroes, she did offer this advice: "Instead of following someone else's heroic life, create one of your own and discover your own path. Learn from the stories of heroes and heroines who have come before us, especially as they teach us to aim high." Now, I like that philosophy of daring to live as the hero in your own story, rather than merely emulating another's.

At the University of California-Berkeley's recent graduation, students were asked to name their heroes—personal or famous—and what they found inspiring about those people. This was apparently a tougher question than usual, and many demurred. However, a clear favorite emerged among those willing to respond: Mom, with other family members right behind her. One such graduate was Janibel: "I have always had a hero: my mother. That hero has never changed. She is a strong, independent woman with the strength to overcome obstacles."[3]

Now, I doubt whether this particular mom is famous. And later in her statement Janibel said her mom is definitely not rich. Yet she is a hero. Even if you and I wouldn't have her on our lists (since we probably don't know her), she is a hero in her daughter's life story.

In the drama that is your life, are you playing your role of the hero—the leading lady? Or are you content to be the understudy—always in the background studying everyone else's lines? Recently, during one of our famous New England snowstorms, my two daughters and I settled down in front of a roaring fire and watched a "chick flick," *The Holiday*. In one very telling scene, a single journalist from London named Iris (played by Kate Winslet) is bemoaning her tendencies toward unrequited love to an elderly screenwriter friend named Arthur (Eli Wallach). As she goes on and on about how she has carried the torch for a real jerk who is engaged to someone else, Arthur interrupts her and declares, "In every film actresses play either leading lady or the best friend. Your problem is that you're meant to be the leading lady, and you've been playing the role of best friend."

Iris, who has spent the last few weeks watching Arthur's recommended old movies about strong, empowered women, finally gets it: "I can't tell you how many years I've been in therapy, and yet you've just explained it. I'm meant to be the leading lady!" From then on, she takes charge of her life story and tells the jerk to get lost and go back to his fiancé while she moves forward with her own life.[4]

Ten years ago as summer turned into fall, two leading ladies died and were mourned by the world. During Labor Day weekend, news came that a great servant of the Lord had gone home to glory—Mother Teresa of Calcutta. But her death was eclipsed by another event that day—the poignant funeral of England's Princess Diana, tragically killed in an automobile accident earlier that week. Needless to say, the worldwide media was consumed by the juxtaposition of the deaths of these two famous people—both heroines but from vastly different lifestyles.

Truly both women were princesses—Diana was England's Rose and Princess of Wales; Mother Teresa was the daughter of the King of kings and princess of the poor and dying. Diana was young and beautiful; Mother Teresa was old and plain looking, but her countenance was radiant in reflecting Christ's love. Malcolm Muggeridge called this *Something Beautiful for God*, the title of his biography of Mother Teresa. Princess Diana's beauty was portrayed on more covers of magazines than any other woman in history.

But I remember hearing her lament in one of her rare interviews, "I just want to be loved." Diana's life story included eating disorders, a very public divorce, and several love affairs. It appeared that no matter how many charities she served or grand openings she attended, she could never quite get enough adulation to make her feel "good enough." How sad that she might have died at age thirty-six feeling that no one truly loved her.

Mother Teresa began the Sisters of Charity in 1950 when she sought permission from Rome to start an order of sisters to serve those "who, crushed by want and destitution, live in conditions unworthy of human dignity." Because she found her ultimate identity as God's beloved daughter, Mother Teresa was able to spend her whole life loving others—especially the unlovely and hard to love—from her place of security in God's love. When she won the Nobel Peace Prize, someone asked her how best to promote world peace. Her answer? "Go home and love your family." Mother Teresa's testimony of love in action was evident throughout her own life story of eighty-seven years.

As I said, both of these women were famous but for different reasons. And both would probably say that fame did not bring them happiness. I will say one thing for both these women—they lived their life stories. They decided to go for it. They didn't sit back and let life happen to them. All too often this is what we do. We want to be heroes, but we don't want to leave our comfortable positions on the sofa in order to do it. So we settle for armchair living.

Armchair Living

On a particular weeknight, 37 million people will drop whatever they're doing, forsake all relational interaction, and stay glued to their TV sets for an hour watching ten very amateur young people compete for top pop singer on *American Idol*.

Thirty-seven million.

And they will do this once or twice every week all spring until the winner is announced! In the meantime, each one of those 37 million people will become attached to the stories of the contestants and will probably develop a favorite for whom they will vote and campaign, and they'll discuss the contest with their friends and coworkers. The *American Idol* phenomenon has been mushrooming in intensity for the past six seasons. Even now, quite early in the competition, distinct personalities and backstories have arisen that propel viewers to blog and debate about certain contestants.

In past seasons, people have gone so far as to call themselves "Claymates" (fans of Clay Aiken) and "Soul Patrol" (fans of Taylor Hicks). Scandals about contestants who posed nude on the Internet, dallied with judges, or broke the law have emerged. There have also been the heartwarming stories of those who overcame adversity to make it this far—the single mom, the war vet, and the surgery survivor who was supposed to lose his voice forever. Everybody has a story, and it seems the American public is more than eager to latch on to someone else's story and never let go.

Isn't that what's behind the current rage of reality TV? We are consumed with other people's stories. One night, you can watch teams of ordinary people rush all over the world on a mammoth scavenger hunt in *The Amazing Race*. And the next, you can view award-winning ballroom dancers paired with B list celebrities perform on *Dancing with the Stars*. By midweek, try critiquing young beauties on *America's Next Top Model* or teams of mismatched adventurers who seek to outwit, outplay, and outlast each other on shows such as *Survivor* and *The Apprentice*. Be inspired by the overcoming stories of weight loss on *The Biggest Loser* or family need on *Extreme Makeover—Home Edition*. Then there's always love and lust matches on shows like *The Bachelor* and *Beauty and the Geek*. Oh yeah, I almost forgot that marriage and parenting are now the subject in shows such as *Nanny 911* and *Wife Swap*. (Since we don't have cable, I had to look up these titles on the Internet.)

The list of reality shows seems endless because the TV public has a seemingly endless need to live vicariously through someone else. (At this point, I must make a confession to being sucked in to more than a few episodes of both *Idol* and *Dancing*.)

That's what I call armchair living. Don't get involved. Don't try to sing, dance, lose weight, or discipline your own kids *yourself*—let someone else do it! Then you will have all the enjoyment of the experience with none of the risk, pain, embarrassment, or, dare I say it, benefits! But not living is exactly that—slowly dying. Stagnation. Lethargy. Coasting. Settling. Yes, getting out of the armchair is risky. And it's vulnerable to throw yourself into the thick of things with no guarantees about the outcome. Relationships, dreams, faith—all these require an element of moving forward with your whole heart!

C. S. Lewis observed, "It would seem that Our Lord finds our desires, not too strong, but too weak. We are half-hearted creatures, fooling about with drink and sex and ambition when infinite joy is offered us, like an ignorant child who wants to go on making mud pies in a slum because he cannot imagine what is meant by the offer of a holiday at the sea. We are far too easily pleased."[5]

To dare to live your story you must not be too easily pleased; you can't merely sit there. A few years ago I heard Charles Colson tell the amazing story of Larry Walters, a thirty-three-year-old man who decided he wanted to see his neighborhood from a new perspective. He went to the local army surplus store one morning and bought forty-five used weather balloons. That afternoon he strapped himself into a lawn chair, to which several of his friends tied the now helium-filled balloons. He took along a peanut butter and jelly sandwich and a BB gun, figuring he could shoot the balloons one at a time when he was ready to land.

Walters, who assumed the balloons would lift him about one hundred feet, was caught off guard when the chair soared to more than eleven thousand feet—smack into the middle of the air traffic pattern at Los Angeles International Airport. Too frightened to shoot any of the balloons, he stayed airborne for more than two hours, forcing the airport to shut down its runways for much of the afternoon, causing long delays in flights from across the country. Soon after he was safely grounded and cited by the police, reporters asked him three questions:

"Were you scared?"

"Yes"

"Would you do it again?"

"No"

"Why did you do it?"

"Because you can't just sit there."

While I don't advocate tying helium balloons to your armchair, I do encourage you to do whatever it takes to propel you headlong into life. Someone once told me, "If you do what you've always done, you'll have what you've always had. But if you want what you've never had, you must do what you've never done."

Jesus said, "I have come that they may have life and have it in abundance" (John 10:10b). *The Message* paraphrase puts it this way: "I came so they can have real and eternal life, more and better life than they ever dreamed of."

Autopilot Living

Another hindrance for living a full life is the tendency to make the journey on autopilot. Early airplanes required the continuous attention of a pilot in order to fly in a safe manner. But in 1914, Lawrence Sperry invented the autopilot system, proving its efficacy by flying the plane with his hands *off the controls*. To this day, increased technology allows aircraft to fly straight and level on a compass course without a pilot's attention, covering more than 80 percent of the workload on a typical flight. I suppose this is not a very comforting thought when we're on a plane—we're at the mercy of machines and computers!

One of the reasons for the invention of the autopilot was to address the fatigue factor in pilots. And that's also what I hear from people who find themselves coasting through life—they are plain worn out. This is especially true of those of us middle aged and beyond. Sometimes it feels like too much effort to learn a new computer program, try a new recipe, or take a short-term mission trip. So we stick with

the same old same old and then wonder why we feel so unfulfilled and useless.

Recently I watched a film called *Stranger Than Fiction*,
and it was indeed strange. An ordinary IRS man, Harold
Crick (played by Will Ferrell) hears a narrator in his head—
the voice of an author (Emma Thompson) making up a story
about his life. She's trying to find a way to wrap up the story
and kill off the main character—him! Eventually she settles
on a conclusion to her novel, but he finds her and begs her
not to kill him off. That is, until he reads the noble way she
plans to do it. His friend, a professor (Dustin Hoffman), tries
to be philosophical and says, "It's the nature of all tragedies.
The hero dies, but the story goes on forever."

For twelve long years Harold has lived on autopilot—
brushing his teeth, setting his watch, and catching the bus
in the exact same way at the exact same time every single
day. Finally, faced with his imminent demise, he is forced to
begin making the life he's always wanted. And so he falls in
love, changes his habits, and breaks out of his mold. That's
why it's especially poignant when he solemnly agrees to play
out his life story in the manner the author has planned. Only
now the author realizes that a man who would willingly die
(when he could have changed the script) is precisely the
sort of man to keep around. We viewers are left to wonder,
*Will she change the story? Or will everyone involved realize the
importance of embracing his unique role, appreciating this gift
called life?*

As the ending unfolds, the narrator continues her chronicle: "Sometimes when we lose ourselves in fear and despair,
in routine and constancy, in hopelessness and tragedy, we can
still find reassurance in a familiar hand on ours or a kind and
loving gesture or a subtle encouragement or a loving embrace
or an offer of comfort."[6]

Do you want to go from living small to living large? My brilliant friend and radio journalist Lael Arrington is from Texas, where everyone lives large! She encourages people not to settle for a system of beliefs that gives only a window on the way the world works: "What we long for is the largeness of Life. . . . God's invitation to play a significant role in His Story is offered to the quiet life as well as to a life with a little more noise. What matters is how we respond—how our vision and passion for God touches a circle of people and rip-ples through eternity. . . . The thing about a story is it invites you to *participate* in that world."[7]

What's keeping you from fully participating in God's story? Are you too busy, and, if so, busy doing what and with whom? Are you too afraid, and, if so, will you let that fear reduce you to a life of inaction and impotence? Are you too ashamed, and, if so, what will it take to convince you that God wants to heal you and use you in His kingdom?

In Boston there is a statue of Phillips Brooks, probably best known for penning the hymn "O Little Town of Bethlehem." But this man was also an author and clergyman, and there is a Phillips Brooks House in Harvard Yard, dedicated in 1900 "to serve the ideal of piety, charity, and hospitality." He would probably be glad to know that today it is the headquarters of student volunteer groups.

More than a century ago, this author and educator warned that the greatest danger we face is not that we will fail or become outright vicious or even be unhappy, finding life meaningless: "The danger is that we may fail to perceive life's *greatest* meaning, fall short of its *highest* good, miss its deepest and most abiding happiness, be unable to ren-der the most needed service, be unconscious of life ablaze with the light of the presence of God—and be content to have it so—that is the danger. That is what one prays one's friends may be spared—satisfaction with life that falls short of the best."

Do you want to miss the mark and be, as Brooks said, "content to have it so"? Not me! I don't want to miss the role of a lifetime that could be mine to play in the great drama of life. Especially not because I'm eating popcorn in front of the TV. Or sharing a stale story of God's working in my life . . . but not recently.

In Lael's fine book *Godsight,* she warns that we will never know what we could experience of God, His people, or His adventure until we actively respond to His invitation: "How can we tell if we're living small? If our escapes and diversions are really costing us? If they are softly becoming the things we love and desire more than God?" It begins with small steps of disobedience. "A heart divided between my dreams and God's dreams. Nothing is smaller than life on a short chain of addiction to anything we love more than God."[8]

Adventurous Living

At the beginning of this chapter the epigraph proclaims, "You are a story." Do you believe that? Dan Allender, in his book *To Be Told,* purported that this understanding is the centerpiece for adventurous living: "The weight of those words, if you believe them even for brief snippets of time, *can change the trajectory of your life!*" Do you believe them? Helen Keller—deaf, dumb, and blind—did and she said, "Life is either a daring adventure, or nothing at all."

All of my children are adventurous. Through the years that has been for me both a source of pride and a source of prayer. To this day, my son Tim (the Eagle Scout) will leak stories of his adventures helicopter skiing in northwestern Canada or climbing the face of the Grand Teton. Though I knew he did these things, I often discover the finer points of harrowing near misses when he laughs about it with his siblings. As he sees my shocked expression, he sheepishly says, "Oh yeah, Mama, I forgot to tell you about that when it happened. I didn't want you to worry." Yeah, right.

Recently my daughter Fiona was giving a presentation on her two-plus years of service with the Peace Corps in the West African country of Guinea. During the question-and-answer session, she calmly remarked about how she had been so sick with malaria the first year. Oops! And that was how Mom and Dad learned of it—in the audience with everyone else. Of course, we had just gone through a nail-biting month while she was being evacuated during a particularly violent political upheaval in Guinea. Still, I'm glad that all my children choose lives that are adventurous and risky, pushing the bounds of comfort. I will admit, though, it's one thing for me to write books about adventurous living and another thing to support Justin, Tim, Fiona, and Maggie in living that way!

Gary Haugen experienced a change in his life story thirteen years ago while he was working as a lawyer for the U.S. Department of Justice. At the height of the genocide in Rwanda, he was loaned to the United Nations to direct an international team of lawyers, criminal prosecutors, law enforcement officers, and forensics experts in gathering evidence against the perpetrators. This Harvard graduate was so moved by his experiences there that he felt compelled to form the International Justice Mission, an organization dedicated to bringing immediate relief to victims of violence and oppression around the world and to pursuing prosecution of perpetrators who abused power to violate and suppress the weak.

Haugen and his team live self-proclaimed dangerous lives: "Loving needy people, it turns out, is not safe. It is uncomfortable. It's messy. It's difficult and scary. Yet paradoxically, Jesus tells us this is where the deepest joy is. And I think it's true."[9]

The short list of what God requires of any adventurer can be found in Micah 6:8: "He has told you men what is good and what it is the LORD requires of you: Only to act justly, to love faithfulness, and to walk humbly with your God." In order to do this, overseas staff members of the International Justice Mission have to let go of comfort, security, control, and success. But in exchange they receive adventure, faith, real miracles, and a deeper walk with Christ.

Would you like to move from armchair and autopilot living into adventurous living? Would you like to embrace your role as the hero in your own life story that is truly part of God's great kingdom story? Where do you begin? Ironically, Gary Haugen would "recommend that we begin by actually doing less and reflecting and praying more: about the life we are living, about the anxieties we carry, about the life we sense God is calling us to live. Search the promises of scripture and take a risk; *live as if these promises were actually true*. Embark on the lifelong journey of spiritual formation and renovation of the heart. It takes reformation of the heart to be brave."[10]

Will we respond to the call of adventurous living? If so, we must give it our all—100 percent for the kingdom of God. "God's real-life action heroes enter His adventure training school and never look back. They train every part of their being—mind, body and soul—to facilitate the supernatural work of God's Spirit within them. And the result is a vibrant, victorious, world-changing life that Hollywood cannot hope to imitate."[11]

"Then I heard the voice of the Lord saying: Who should I send? Who will go for Us? I said: Here I am. Send me" (Isa. 6:8).

⇀ **My Life Story** ⇀

Who are your heroes?
- Biblical:

- Literary:

- Modern-day:

- Spiritual:

What characteristics stand out in each of these people?

Name one time when you said, "Yes!" and it totally changed your life. Describe the outcome.

Try writing your life story in five sentences. I thought this would be so hard, but then I sat down and wrote. Here are my unedited answers.

1. I grew up in a small Georgia town with two sisters and loving parents who encouraged me to become all that God called me to be.
2. As a young adult I earned several degrees, enjoyed a variety of friends, and traveled around the world twice through my work in both journalism and Christian ministry.
3. Most of my adult life, even while struggling with a variety of issues, I used the gifts God gave me through communication—writing and speaking to encourage others.
4. Marrying Mike and becoming a mother of four were both the greatest joys in my life and the calling that most required God's grace, wisdom, and guidance.
5. Because of my many sins of both commission and omission, I live each day under God's mercy and utter faithfulness through His constant presence, bountiful provision, and incomparable power in my life's journey.

Your turn.
1.

2.

3.

4.

5.

He has told you men [and women] what is good
and what it is the Lord requires of you:
Only to act justly, to love faithfulness,
and to walk humbly with your God.
Micah 6:8

Chapter 5

The Villain

One of the things that surprised me when I first read
the New Testament seriously was that it talked so much about
a Dark Power in the universe—a mighty evil spirit who was held
to be the Power behind death, disease and sin. . . .
Christianity agrees this is a universe at war.
C. S. Lewis, *Mere Christianity*

I don't consider myself controversial. I speak. I write. I challenge people to go deeper in their faith with the God who gives them grace and mercy. My style is approachable, content-driven, and humorous even when I don't mean to be. Before every event I pray that God will use me and fill me with His Spirit and that each listener will walk away with at least one nugget of potentially life-changing truth. I don't consider this a very living-on-the-edge kind of work. But, in actuality, my lifestyle is not merely controversial, it is dangerous.

Still, I never expected to be attacked.

It was a beautiful autumn evening in a particularly pleasant part of the country (not my own state), and I was delighted to be speaking on the subject of "Tea and Friendship." This was one of those outreach events to which church ladies invite their friends, neighbors, and coworkers for an evening of inspiration and beauty—precisely the pick-me-up needed by today's overworked and underappreciated woman on the go. We had a good crowd, and my host had already attached the wireless microphone to my suit jacket. Immediately after her introduction, I stood to begin my presentation. To my astonishment, from the middle of the large crowd a woman stood up tall and angry and began screaming nasty accusatory words at me—maligning my character, my witness, and my integrity.

I was absolutely shocked. But even though it took me off guard, I sensed immediately what was behind this tirade. It seemed incredulous, but this person was attacking me because I had been a witness for the defense at a trial *two years before*. The legal judgments had been served and resolved, but the acrimony had evidently not abated. While others involved suffered needlessly and hoped to move beyond, this night in this town, I happened to be the target of rage.

The seconds it took for me to react were quicker than the time it took for you to read the above explanation. I owe that to the power of the Holy Spirit, filling me with wisdom and courage, for, in truth I was shaking all over. But I was wired for sound! I immediately began singing at the top of my lungs Martin Luther's "A Mighty Fortress Is Our God," encouraging the group to join me.

Together we sang with power, drowning out the protestor:

And though this world with devils filled, should threaten to undo us,

We will not fear, for God has willed His truth to triumph through us.

The Prince of darkness grim, we tremble not for him.

His rage we can endure, for, lo, his doom is sure.

One little word shall fell him.

By the end of that stanza, the police had been called and the woman had been escorted out in deference to an existing restraining order. I took a deep breath. Then I took another. And when I couldn't stop my racing heart, I finally said, "Let us pray."

Then I proceeded to give my inspirational talk on "Tea and Friendship." No joke. To this day I cannot believe that God gave me words and presence of mind to make it through because I kept shaking for at least the first half of the talk. But He did. Words of encouragement and hope were shared as well as tea and treats. Who would have thought that my support for a friend would be the most significant, unspoken illustration of my subject? Later, at the book table, some of the attendees said they thought at first that I had "planted" a heckler merely to start things off with a bang. Yeah, right.

There is a villain in our life story. There is an enemy of our souls. And he will do whatever is necessary to get us off track, to prevent us from living the unique role that God has planned for each of us in helping to further His kingdom here on earth. You say I'm being overly dramatic? Believe it. Please believe that we are at war.

Accusations

The villain in your story wants to win. He wants to make your life so miserable, so full of fear, confusion, worry, and doubt that you will simply become paralyzed and unable to move forward in any kind of productive and redeeming way. If he can immobilize you, if he can demoralize you, if he can distract you from the role God has cast you in, he will have accomplished his purpose.

Writing this book has been a case in point. Ever since signing the contract, I've been tempted to succumb to his wiles. First came the niggling doubt: *Whatever made you believe you could write a book that would help people move from the mundane to the magnificent, anyway?* Then a frontal assault: *After all, you're not exactly living to the fullest a particularly enviable or exemplary life yourself, now are you?* And finally, a cut to the jugular: *Ha! You call your ministry Encouraging Words and you haven't even been able to write a word for two months now!* OK, OK, I know that seems true. *Gotcha!*

When has he said, "Gotcha!" to you lately? In your marriage? In your parenting? At work? In your volunteer ministry at church? In your relationships? At school? One thing you can be sure of: the devil knows precisely the right place to attack. He knows where you are most vulnerable and when. And that's exactly how and where he will strike. "Pay careful attention, then, to how you walk—not as unwise people but as wise—making the most of the time, because the days are evil" (Eph. 5:15–16).

If you want a particularly good visual on this, consider the opening scene of the powerful film *The Passion of the Christ*. Jesus (James Caviezel) is alone in the Garden of Gethsemane, literally sweating drops of blood over the impending role He has been called by God to play. He is at his most vulnerable. His disciples seem clueless (even with all the Last Supper hints) and have all fallen asleep. This is the very time that Satan (a cloaked androgynous figure) appears and hisses out condemnation and reproach.[1]

His accusations definitely come when we're most vulnerable, but don't think the enemy always looks scary and menacing. Satan is far more subtle. In fact, one of my friends declares, "He comes to us like Diane Sawyer, so understanding, wanting our story, laughing at the right moments, blue eyes sparkling, blond hair shining, tearing up at the right moments. Digging out our resentment and hurt in an unguarded moment. Inviting us to vent just a little for the camera."[2]

My friend Susan Duke was assaulted by the enemy at her lowest point, immediately after her teenage son, Thomas, was killed in an accident. She can certainly testify that Satan loves to torment us in our most vulnerable times. In her first throes of grief, these taunting phrases pierced her soul.

"Heartsong Ministries?" the jeering began. *"That's over. You don't have a song in your heart now, do you? And you never will again. You think you were called to give joy to people? Well, where is your joy now? Do you think you'll ever feel joy again? I think not! Where was God when you needed Him today? He let your son die. Your ministry is over. Your joy is over. Your life is over. Everything you've ever trusted and believed in is a lie."*[3]

Have you heard such sneering whispers? Have you believed them? Susan recalls that at the time she felt too physically and emotionally weak to fight the enemy on her own, even though she had the presence of mind to realize that she was in a life-and-death battle. Would she believe the lies of darkness, or would she find the strength to hold on tightly to the truth she had discovered while in the light?

While we may not all have mourned the death of a child, most of us have found ourselves at a low point when the tide could turn either way. Either we buy into all the accusations and believe the lies that nothing will ever change, or we summon the strength to hold on to what we know is true (even if it doesn't *feel* true at the time) and we stand firm.

As she elaborated in her excellent book *Grieving Forward,* Susan was able to supernaturally pull herself up, clench her fist, and shout into the darkness, "You've made the wrong mama mad! If I believe anything I've read in God's Word or any of the words I've sung, then I believe that my son is with the Lord. I will see him again. Hear me now! As long as I have breath, I will sing. And I will speak. And as long as I live, Thomas's life will have meaning and change lives."[4]

"He will bring me into the light; I will see His salvation. Then my enemy will see, and she will be covered with shame, the one who said to me, 'Where is the LORD your God?' My eyes will look at her in triumph; at that time she will be trampled like mud in the streets" (Mic. 7:9b–10).

Apathy

But sometimes it's easier to fight the taunting than it is to fight the apathy. Other times the apathy comes because we believe the accusations:

- "I can't begin to write this book, so I may as well sit in front of the TV and watch hours and hours of *Masterpiece Theatre*."
- "I just really don't *feel* like writing today, and besides, who's going to miss my book anyway?"
- "I think I'll start working on chapter outlines next week after the wedding/play/conference/holiday/crisis is over. Yeah, that's what I'll do—wait until nothing else is going on."

How many ways have you justified apathy lately? It's a lot more comfortable to coast through a life than to engage in a life, isn't it?

In C. S. Lewis's *The Screwtape Letters*, the Devil meets with his underdevils to plan how best to combat Christianity. Each underdevil is assigned the challenge to come up with a catchy slogan. One suggests, "There is no God." The Devil feels this would be hard to promote. Another suggests, "There is no devil." Again the idea is rejected as not possible. The last little devil comes up with the slogan, "There is no hurry." The perfect slogan to defeat Christianity!

How would that strategy work for you? You wouldn't be reading this book unless you wanted your life to count for something, unless you were willing to make a difference in

God's kingdom. So could you be sidetracked by the "There's no hurry" syndrome? It is far too easy for Christ's followers to settle down into false security and think that what we see is all there is. We would be wrong. There is an unseen world full of activity, and much of it is targeted at us! That's why we must use wisdom, prayer, and action to ward off evil. "The weapons of our warfare are not fleshly, but are powerful through God for the demolition of strongholds. We demolish arguments and every high-minded thing that is raised up against the knowledge of God, taking every thought captive to the obedience of Christ" (2 Cor. 10:4–5).

Several of my creative author friends battle against enemies they have actually named. Bonnie Keen calls her Lois, the voice that always criticizes her and calls into question her decisions and her trust in God. I don't know how Bonnie came up with that name, but the concept works, especially when Bonnie uses video of Lois (who looks like Bonnie but has another voice) cajoling and trying to trick her. This repartee in a presentation helps the audience see the battle that takes place within ourselves. How can we be apathetic and ignore this kind of behavior?

Even the apostle Paul admitted his struggle:

For we know that the law is spiritual; but I am made out of flesh, sold into sin's power. For I do not understand what I am doing, because I do not practice what I want to do, but I do what I hate. And if I do what I do not want to do, I agree with the law that it is good. So now I am no longer the one doing it, but it is sin living in me. For I know that nothing good lives in me, that is, in my flesh. For the desire to do what is good is with me, but there is no ability to do it. For I do not do the good that I want to do, but I practice the evil that I do not want to do.

Now if I do what I do not want, I am no longer the
one doing it, but it is the sin that lives in me. So I
discover this principle: when I want to do good, evil
is with me. For in my inner self I joyfully agree with
God's law. But I see a different law in the parts of my
body, waging war against the law of my mind and
taking me prisoner to the law of sin in the parts of
my body. (Rom. 7:14–23)

Another friend, Joanna Weaver, has aptly named her
sin nature Flesh Woman. Now there's a term I can relate to!
Flesh Woman is

that contrary, rebellious, incredibly self-centered
version of you who shows up when things don't
go the way you planned and life seems habitually
unfair. . . . [She's the] righteous indignation we use
to justify our not-so-righteous anger. The flattery we
pour on in order to secure coveted positions. The
false humility in which we cloak ourselves while
secretly hoping to be admired. Unfortunately, we
rarely pause to wonder if what we're doing is wrong.
And that's just where Flesh Woman wants it to be.
For if you were to pull off her mask, you'd know
what she's really up to. Her main goal is not your
benefit, but her power base. Though Flesh Woman
would never admit it, she's determined to do whatever it takes to remain in control of your life.[5]

Think how the story of the Israelites could have been
different if not for apathy and giving in to fear. Remember
how during the exodus they sent twelve spies to have a look
at the Promised Land? But ten of them returned, conclud-
ing something like this: "Let's stay in the safety of our camp
rather than venturing forth on a wing and a prayer. Who
knows what danger lies ahead?" Only Joshua and Caleb were

captured by the vision of what could be, so they urged the Israelites to press on and take the land. But their voices were drowned out by those who succumbed to apathy generated by the ten faithless spies.

And Israel wandered in the wilderness for another forty years. Forty years! Do you and I really have another forty years to sit around, wringing our hands and lamenting that things will never change? I think not.

In our life stories, the villain is after us through voices of condemnation and accusation and through wearying us of the struggle so that we throw up our hands in apathetic surrender. In light of this, we need to prepare ourselves and be armed for the battle.

Armed for Battle

In the epigraph at the beginning of this chapter, C. S. Lewis is quoted: "Christianity agrees this is a universe at war." Frankly, I'm not at all sure that "Christianity agrees" on that statement. Most of the Christians I encounter don't act at all as though they are fighting a battle between the forces of good and the forces of evil. We are ill prepared and taken by ambush. Then we whine, bemoan our failings, and call ourselves victims. Why not fight back? Why not summon all the strength we can muster and charge into life full force?

A few years ago at the International Christian Retail Show in Denver, I attended an event when author John Eldredge was presented with an award for selling gazillions of books. The publisher presented to him a large sword, certainly as big as the one his *Braveheart* hero William Wallace used in Scotland many years ago. John loved it, as it was truly representative of his belief that all believers must be prepared to do battle for their very lives. The author of such books as *The Sacred Romance* and *Waking the Dead* boldly stated, "We are at war. This is a Love Story set in the midst of a life and death battle. Look around you at all the casualties strewn across the fields, the lost souls, the broken hearts, the captives. We must take this battle seriously—it is a war for the human heart. You have a crucial role to play. Many have underestimated their roles in the Story but that is dangerous. You will lose heart and you will miss your cues."[6]

Paul said something similar to the believers at Ephesus when he charged them to be prepared for what was ahead:

Finally, be strengthened by the Lord and by His vast strength. Put on the full armor of God so that you can stand against the tactics of the Devil. For our battle is not against flesh and blood, but against the rulers, against the authorities, against the world powers of this darkness, against the spiritual forces of evil in the heavens. This is why you must take up the full armor of God, so that you may be able to resist in the evil day, and having prepared everything, to take your stand. Stand, therefore, with truth like a belt around your waist, righteousness like armor on your chest, and your feet sandaled with readiness for the gospel of peace. In every situation take the shield of faith, and with it you will be able to extinguish the flaming arrows of the evil one. Take the helmet of salvation, and the sword of the Spirit, which is God's word. With every prayer and request, pray at all times in the Spirit, and stay alert in this, with all perseverance and intercession for all the saints. (Eph. 6:10–18)

The one purpose of the enemy is the destruction of all God loves, particularly His beloved. That's you and me. He stalks us day and night as the Lord tells us through Peter, "Be sober! Be on the alert! Your adversary the Devil is prowling around like a roaring lion, looking for anyone he can devour" (1 Pet. 5:8). Many years ago I was on safari in Kenya, and early one morning we happened upon a kill. Everyone else was thrilled since this was a rare opportunity to see a lion totally destroy a gazelle and eat it alive. Needless to say, it made me sick and even sicker when I realized it was a biblical picture of what the enemy wants to do to me! Fortunately Peter followed up in verse 9 with this admonition: "Resist him, firm in the faith, knowing that the same sufferings are being experienced by your brothers in the world."

We must be armed for battle. Each of us must find the courage to rise up and fight for ourselves and for others in this Kingdom. But never forget that the King of kings is leading us on and preparing the way: "'I will go before you and level the uneven places; I will shatter the bronze doors and cut the iron bars in two. I will give you the treasures of darkness and riches from secret places, so that you may know that I, the LORD, the God of Israel call you by your name'" (Isa. 45:2–3).

Ken Gire gave us this charge: "We resist the enemy by fervently loving the Lord Jesus, by fiercely trusting Him, by faithfully serving Him. As members of the resistance movement, boldly we pray, bravely we fight. For He is the King. The one true King. And He's worth fighting for."[7]

⟶ My Life Story ⟵

When Satan whispers accusations in your ear, what does he say?

What do you do to fight apathy in your own life? Next time you don't feel like moving forward, what are practical steps you can take to get out of your rut?

If you are a warrior princess in the battle between good and evil, what holy armor do you most need today? What will that look like, and how can you attain it?

Pay careful attention, then, to how you walk—
not as unwise people but as wise—making the most
of the time, because the days are evil.
Ephesians 5:15–16

Chapter 6

Backstory

For most of us, life feels like a movie we've arrived at forty-five
minutes late. If there is meaning to this life, then why do our days
seem so *random*? What is this drama we've been dropped into the
middle of? If there is a God, what sort of story is He telling here?
We find ourselves in the middle of a story that is sometimes
wonderful, sometimes awful, often a confusing mixture of both,
and we haven't a clue how to make sense of it all.
It's like we're holding in our hands some pages torn out of a book.
These pages are the days of our lives. Fragments of a story.
They seem important, or at least we long to know they are,
but what does it all mean? If only we could find the book
that contains the rest of the story.
John Eldredge, *Epic*

This is where it all began, I thought as I slowly walked the
brick pathway to the front porch. Climbing the stairs,
I turned, my back to the front door, and gazed at the expanse
of yard beyond me. A lifetime of Easter egg hunts, softball
games, birthday scavenger hunts, kickball, chasing fireflies
(we called them lightnin' bugs), and family photo shoots
flashed through my mind. The landscaping was different—
my mama's meticulously planted flower gardens were gone
now in favor of a practical lawn with simple upkeep, but
the expanse still seemed huge. Yet I was familiar with every

inch—the section of the yard where Barbie and Ken took their camping trips, the corner where my tree house had stood, and the hill where I went sailing out of control while learning to ride a bike ("How do I stop it, Daddy?" were my final words before the crash, I believe). It was all here, and a rush of memories stirred my emotions.

Goodness! I thought. *I'm not even inside yet. I'd better get a grip!*

I turned back to the front door, took a deep breath, and rang the bell. After nearly thirty years, I was returning to the house where I was born and called home my first twenty-five years—Pinecrest. Our land, directly across the street from where my mama had grown up, had been a wedding gift from my maternal grandparents. The new house was built and ready to move into after my folks' honeymoon in 1949. Our family name, Secrest, was combined with the surrounding tall Georgia pine trees to inspire the name Pinecrest.

This was the only home I ever knew as a child. Every rite of passage occurred here—every first step, lost tooth, impossible dream, broken heart, and new adventure had its genesis here. At least for my first twenty-five years.

Since Mama and Daddy moved out, I had visited them and my hometown many times through the years, eventually bringing a husband and four children to drive by "the house where Mama grew up." But I had never made the pilgrimage inside. Until now. Now it was time.

As part of uncovering my own life story, I needed to go home and I needed to do it alone. The current owners—Stephen and Julie—could not have been more gracious or accommodating to my out-of-the-blue request to have a moment in their home. Answering the doorbell, they greeted me with grace and hospitality that confirmed what I had already suspected and fervently hoped—this was a loving family home. Still.

My gasp came as I stepped over the threshold and faced the staircase to my upstairs bedroom. "Why, it's so small!" I exclaimed.

How many times had I and my sisters hovered at the top of the stairs furtively spying on a grown-up party or waiting to be released to the tree on Christmas morning? How vast the living room had seemed back then!

As I began my exploration, I was delighted to discover original doors and cabinets and black-and-white bathroom tile. Yes, the decor was far more elegant than we had ever known, and the clean lines and immaculate display were a sharp contrast to our family's eclectic, collectibles lifestyle. But the essence of our home was still here. Even after thirty years. Stephen and Julie pointed out on the wall a framed pen-and-ink drawing of Pinecrest that my parents had given them.

While it was great to see the whole house and yard, I had a definite destination of primary importance—my little bedroom, top of the stairs and front of the house. As I walked in, I was momentarily taken aback by the masculine furniture and floor-to-ceiling sports awards. This was now home to a star Duke University football player.

But all that faded as I went over to the bed under the window. My eyes filled with tears as I whispered to my hosts, "I saw the whole world from this window." It was true. The bed in that corner had been my haven—my sanctuary from the world, where I would curl up and read voraciously of far-away places, hardly daring to dream that I would one day actually experience them. Or perhaps bury myself in a pillow, crying my eyes out because I felt rejected and unpopular—a nonconformist in a sea of sameness.

There had been hours spent listening to Rod McKuen poetry records and writing my own poems and stories in diaries, wanting somehow to capture meaning in my musings. And this corner, too, was where I read my Bible and memorized favorite verses such as John 14 ("Let not your heart be troubled . . .") and read daily devotions from Mrs. Charles E. Cowman's *Streams in the Desert*.

There were times when I sat on that bed and hated myself because I felt fat and loud and bossy and selfish. And, truth be told, there were plenty of times when I *was* those things. But I think (at least if I squint my eyes and stretch my fifty-plus memory) there were also times when I dared to believe that I was smart and beautiful and adventurous and even capable of being used by God to help change the world. And, incredible as it seems, I really was those things too.

Every time I played the Mamas and the Papas "This is Dedicated to the One I Love" or cradled a doll and sang her to sleep ("Hush, little baby, don't say a word . . ."), I was also dreaming of a life that would include my own family to love. I would be well into my thirties before those blessings would eventually come my way, but that, too, became a fulfilled dream—a gift of God's grace to me.

As I reluctantly bid farewell to my hosts and walked to my rental car, I could almost hear the barks of Frisky, Rusty, Pepper, Cinnamon, Ginger, and Parsley (we had been partial to spices and herbs for dog names) sending me on my way. This had been a happy place, and my memories were good ones. Here I had been nurtured, provided for, taught, prayed for, disciplined, and encouraged to become all that God had for me. Most of all, I had been loved. Mama and Daddy assured me of their love every day of my life, and they still do. *Thank You, God, for this legacy of love You gave me,* I prayed as I drove away.

* * *

In a book or movie, the backstory refers to the history behind the current situation—basically what happened before that sets into motion what is happening now. This literary device, often employed to lend the main story depth or verisimilitude, is done in a variety of ways such as flashback, narration, or character explanations. They hint at mysteries, pivotal moments, or seminal circumstances that altered the whole course of life for a certain character. As the backstory is slowly revealed, we come to a better understanding of why the character acts the way he does. For instance, the third Indiana Jones movie, *Indiana Jones and the Last Crusade*, begins with a scene set during the protagonist Indiana's childhood, explaining how he acquired his hat, his whip, the scar on his chin, and his fear of snakes.[1]

Perhaps one of the most expansive current illustrations of backstory is the very popular musical *Wicked*, which seeks to give the background of the two witches from *The Wizard of Oz*. Long before Dorothy dropped in, two other girls met at witch school in the Land of Oz. Elphaba, born with emerald-green skin, is smart, fiery, and misunderstood. Galinda is beautiful, ambitious, and very popular. How these two unlikely friends end up as the Wicked Witch of the West and Glinda the Good Witch makes for a spellbinding story. While this is totally speculative and not in any way attributed to the original Oz author, L. Frank Baum, it is a conjecture that seeks to give new meaning to what eventually happens in the Land of Oz.

To understand my story I must first know my backstory. I didn't come to have a ministry called Encouraging Words that Transform because my parents put me down all the time. No, their encouragement grew me into an encourager of others. And my own struggles with wanting everyone to like me and everyone to always be happy directly stem from the kind of superficial Southern gentility that pervaded my small town in the early sixties. Radical decisions such as graduating from high school after my junior year were pivotal in how my own story would evolve.

Some of you may have tuned me out by now because your backstory was quite different from mine. Perhaps you don't come from a loving family or secure home life. Perhaps you've suffered such emotional and psychological abuse that you've even suppressed memories of your past. How does that kind of legacy factor into fulfilling your role in life? While I cannot fully understand what you've gone through, I know One who does. "He was despised and rejected by men, a man of suffering who knew what sickness was. . . . Yet He Himself bore our sicknesses, and He carried our pains. . . . He was pierced because of our transgressions, crushed because of our iniquities; punishment for our peace was on Him, and we are healed by His wounds" (Isa. 53:3–5).

No matter what kind of pain and recovery you have gone through, Jesus understands and is the One who wants to bring complete healing in your life. He also knows that you must examine your backstory in order to move forward into the future full of hope that He has for you. (We will examine Joseph's life in this way.) So don't compare your life with others', especially mine, but ask God to show you what's important to know about *your* history so that you can face life with renewed strength.

When Alex Haley published *Roots* back in 1976, he was saying to generations of black people in America, "Your story began *before* the slavery—and it's a rich and wonderful story indeed." We all need to face our own roots and determine how they fit into the story we are living now. "Sooner or later you must go home again. You must face the depths of that well. The parentage, the family story, the tribal story, the story of the hometown or region—all of it contributes to who you are now."[2]

Nowhere is the backstory more important than in Joseph's story, found in the book of Genesis in the Old Testament. Joseph's life took him from pampered son to imprisoned slave to Egyptian ruler. He had a major role in preserving the future of God's people, and yet he was greatly affected by all that had come before his time. I believe we can use Joseph as an example of how to embrace our lives, yes, even in the midst of whatever backstory is ours.

Facing Facts

The first step is to face facts. In other words, what were the circumstances and family relationships like before you came along? Do a little research and ask older family members about significant events, feuds, or setbacks that might have contributed to the atmosphere into which you were born. Were your parents married? Did they go to college? What kind of work did they do? Did they live near their families? Who were their friends? Whether or not you were an only child and even your birth order among siblings can contribute to your view of life.

Joseph's own story, like ours, began long before he was born. His great-grandfather was none other than "Father Abraham," the one to whom God promised his descendents would number more than the stars. But, as Abraham and his wife Sarah became elderly, they still had no children. Taking matters into their own hands, Abraham did have a child—Ishmael—by his servant Hagar. But that was not the fulfillment of God's promise. God did eventually give Abraham and Sarah a son—Isaac. And the enmity between those two sons—Isaac and Ishmael—was the genesis of the Middle Eastern conflict that reigns to this day.

Isaac, Joseph's grandfather, married Rebekah and they also had two sons—Esau and Jacob. But Rebekah convinced her youngest son, Jacob, to trick his father into giving him his older brother's birthright. This act of deception caused murderous estrangement between these two brothers in yet another generation of the family. So Jacob left home and worked for his Uncle Laban (Rebekah's brother) who then, in turn, deceived him by giving him Leah for a bride, rather than Jacob's first choice, Rachel. He then had to work seven more years in order to marry Rachel. Do you see how this backstory of conniving and deceit affected the family unit? And it continued into the new generation when Joseph's own older brothers also tricked the Shechemites (circumcising and killing them all) after they raped the boys' sister, Dinah.

By the time Joseph was born, Jacob had ten other sons through Leah and two servants. But Joseph was his first son with his beloved wife Rachel. Later Rachel died shortly after giving birth to Benjamin. These twelve sons of Jacob were destined to become the twelve tribes of Israel. But first a lot of drama was played out among them. Jacob did indeed love Joseph and Benjamin more than all the rest, and thus Joseph grew up as a pampered and privileged son.

Because Joseph was bright, handsome, and given to interpreting dreams, he acted quite cocky in flaunting his gift from Dad—the coat of many colors. He also freely boasted about his dream in which all his brothers were bowing down to him. None of this won him any popularity contests, and thus he was doomed by circumstances beyond his control. His brothers sold him into slavery, pretended he was killed, and returned the bloody robe to a distraught father. I can't help but wonder, if Joseph had been a bit more keen on family dynamics, would he have made choices that widened the love gap between him and his brothers? Nonetheless, he found himself abandoned and alienated.

On your own journey of discovering and living out your role, it's important to face the facts of your backstory—both those within and beyond your control.

Formative Events

In all our stories, seminal formative events propel us and others on paths that greatly affect our lives. You had the opportunity to name some of these in the chapter 3 "Studying Your Script" exercise, and it's important to reflect on both the choices you made and the consequences of those choices. For Joseph, his first role in slavery was as assistant to Potiphar, and he earned respect and admiration in the household for a job well done: "From the time that he [Potiphar] put him in charge of his household and of all that he owned, the LORD blessed the Egyptian's house because of Joseph. The LORD's blessing was on all that he owned, in his house and in his fields" (39:5). However, some of that adulation came from the boss's wife. When Joseph refused her sexual advances, her retaliatory accusations led to his imprisonment. His only crime was trying to lead a life of integrity, one that honored God.

Where was Joseph's backstory in this new formative event? Well, part of his heritage was a family who trusted in God. Even to this day we hear reference to "the God of Abraham, Isaac, and Jacob." They were not perfect, but they were men who believed in God and His provision and sovereignty in all things. Joseph had this legacy and clung to it despite dire circumstances. Genesis chapter 39 begins and ends with the phrase *"The LORD was with"* Joseph. Later Pharaoh, in looking for someone to govern his people, noticed that Joseph was a man who had "the spirit of God in him" (41:38b).

After years of languishing in prison, he was finally remembered by other prisoners he had helped, and Joseph was called to interpret Pharaoh's disturbing dreams. This gift of dream interpretation (the one that had gotten him into trouble earlier) was once again used in a very formative way in Joseph's life. He not only explained about the pending seven years of prosperity and ensuing seven years of famine, but he also proposed a plan through which Egypt could store and prepare for the coming years. Lo and behold, the pharaoh entrusted him with this task, and Joseph rose to be the most powerful man in all of Egypt: "'Since God has made all this known to you, there is no one as intelligent and wise as you. You will be over my house, and all my people will obey your commands. Only with regard to the throne will I be greater than you.' Pharaoh also said to Joseph, 'See, I am placing you over all the land of Egypt'" (41:39–41).

Talk about a roller-coaster life! Joseph had experienced both the depths and heights of life in his new land. His overarching role was to be a courageous leader to help save people, but God also used his role as a prisoner to prepare him inwardly for what he would need—trust, strength, perseverance, and mercy. Nothing is wasted on our journey in life. It all works together to make us the person we are becoming.

Forward Living

But it's not enough merely to know the details of our backstory and to examine the way we handled formative events in our lives. None of us is chained to the past. While it is important and part of our story, it is not the whole story. God is always doing a new thing. In fact, one sentence I nearly always include in any presentation is: *It is never too late to write a new story of the rest of your life.* If we are truly daring to live the life God carved out for us from the beginning, we must be courageous enough to move forward.

During his very busy fourteen years of administrating Egypt, Joseph had plenty of time to relive the past and plan revenge on his brothers. We have no indication what his thoughts were, but we know that he did not choose to live in the past. Scripture indicates that he got on with his life, married Asenath, and had at least two sons—Manasseh and Ephraim. Yet because he was a man with a special gift of discernment and prophecy, I suspect he knew in his heart that one day he would come face-to-face with his backstory. What would he choose then? Would he give in and get even, or would he rise above and reconcile?

Most of our histories include both good and bad. Even though some people find their identity in going through life as a victim, none of us are truly doomed to live defined merely by what others have (or have not) done to us. Even Joseph's ancestors worked at reconciliation. His own father, Jacob, and Uncle Esau had a dramatic reconciliation because each of them was courageous enough to move forward in the relationship rather than staying paralyzed by past sins and prejudice. When Esau rushed to welcome him, Jacob replied to the healing gesture, "For indeed, I have seen your face, and it is like seeing God's face, since you have accepted me. Please take my present that was brought to you, because God has been gracious to me and I have everything I need" (33:10b–11).

In his heart Joseph wanted reconciliation with his brothers, but a part of him used a bit of trickery to keep the upper hand. Because of the famine, the ten older brothers went to Egypt and bowed before the ruler, asking for food for their extended family, never suspecting that the person they were bowing down to was their own brother! And Joseph was startled to see his childhood dreams literally come true right before his eyes! He accused his brothers of being spies and required they bring back their younger brother to prove their good intent. While the brothers conversed and decided that this was the price they were paying for selling Joseph so long ago, unbeknownst to them, Joseph understood and retreated to cry over the situation.

His brothers returned with Benjamin, but they were frightened since all their silver brought as a gift to Joseph had been replaced in their food sacks. Then Joseph inquired of the health of their father, and when he saw Benjamin, he was again so overcome with weeping that he had to leave the room (43:30). Once again he tricked his brothers by hiding a silver cup in Benjamin's sack, and they broke down and declared they could never return home without their youngest brother; it would simply kill their father since he had already lost one favorite son (chap. 44).

At that point Joseph could stand it no longer. He cleared the room of everyone except his brothers, stood, and declared to them, "I am Joseph," which terrified the men even more. "'I am Joseph, your brother,' he said, 'the one you sold into Egypt. And now don't be worried or angry with yourselves for selling me here, because God sent me ahead of you to preserve life. For the famine has been in the land these two years, and there will be five more years without plowing or harvesting. God sent me ahead of you to establish you as a remnant within the land and to keep you alive by a great deliverance. Therefore it was not you who sent me here, but God. He has made me a father to Pharaoh, lord of his entire household, and ruler over all the land of Egypt'" (45:4b–8).

Joseph sent for his father, Jacob, and settled his entire family of seventy "in the land of Egypt, in the region of Goshen. They acquired property in it and became fruitful and very numerous" (47:27). The entire family was once again reunited, and it looked as though the story would have a happy ending. But when the patriarch died, the brothers were worried that Joseph would then take his revenge. Instead, Joseph assured them, "You planned evil against me; God planned it for good to bring about the present result—the survival of many people" (50:20).

What a testimony of how God can take the evil works of people and use even those to bring about the story He wants to write in the life of a person willing to be used of Him. I have talked to countless people who hold on to this chronicle in hope if they find themselves falsely accused, imprisoned, deceived, or alone in a foreign land. I truly believe that Joseph dared to live his unique story by staying faithful to God each step of the way and trusting Him for a future he could not predict.

As you think about the backstory of your life, offer both the good and bad elements to God, and ask Him to help you discern their part in your ongoing story. Face the facts, and then make good choices during formative events that can literally make or break you, and always determine that you will not be chained to a past but will go forward in life with courage and strength exactly as Joseph did.

⟶ My Life Story ⟵

Picture the house you grew up in (if several houses, choose the one you lived in when you were ten years old). On a separate piece of paper, draw a rough floor plan of that house as though you were looking down from above. Try to especially remember details from important rooms such as your bedroom, the family room, or kitchen.

What was your favorite place in this home, and why do you remember it so vividly?

Robert L. Morgan in *Remembering Your Story* said, "In remembering life in our family of origin and the stories that often are kept hidden in closets and closed minds, we discover the forces that made us what we are today, helping put our lives in perspective. . . . Our early family is a critical key to who we are now."

How did your parents meet?

How did their families feel about the marriage (or no marriage if they weren't wed)?

Describe the family unit you were born into (parents' ages and vocations, siblings, house/apartment, church and community involvement, socioeconomic status, etc.).

What values were considered most important in your family?

Vinita Hampton Wright in *The Soul Tells a Story* warned, "Your origins might be delightful—or they might be filled with horror. Give them the names they deserve, but work at facing them. . . . Once you have looked at your origins head-on, called them what you would and accepted their existence in your life, you will have more liberty to pursue what comes next."

Are you aware today of any long-ago family secrets? What were they?

What was your family's greatest strength?

Greatest weakness?

Complete these sentences:

"One of my happiest family memories is when . . ."

"An especially difficult time in our family was when . . ."

You planned evil against me;
God planned it for good to bring about the present result—
the survival of many people.
Genesis 50:20

Chapter 7

The Plot Thickens

All noble things are difficult.
Living in the invisible kingdom is a heroic and holy thing.
But the difficulty of it does not make us give up; it inspires us
to overcome because our suffering is not wasteful. It counts for
something that what we are going through is strengthening us in
a way that helps us. The King will continue to supply us with the
courage and the grace not only to survive, but to grow stronger.
Nicole Johnson, *Having a Princess Heart*

Life gets messy. At times you may hear words like these:

- Your medical diagnosis is clinical depression.
- We don't know why, but he was born with mental retardation.
- Your husband needs an emergency five-way heart bypass . . . tomorrow.
- This is the bank calling about your account.
- He's in the hospital and almost died from alcohol poisoning.
- I'm calling to schedule a mammogram follow-up, for more tests.
- Because of violence, she's being evacuated to the nearest safe country.
- Your father has a brain tumor . . . again.

- She scored way too high on the psychologist's stress test.
- These poor health choices are slowly killing you.
- No financial aid or scholarships are available at this time.
- Some people die from this operation.
- Your best friend left you a suicide note.

Yes, life gets messy, and your life story can change dramatically as the plot thickens. Often one simple phrase can send you reeling. I know that each of the above sentences profoundly changed my script and sent me running to the Director for editing tips! Because not only is life messy, but it catches you off guard. You start out thinking that if you follow a certain script, all will fall into place on that road to happily ever after. But that would be dull, wouldn't it? And, after all, the best stories are all about overcoming adversity.

"What is a movie without conflict? Where's the drama without a mountain of impossibility to climb? The very thing that makes for an exciting story is the same thing that makes for a wonderful and amazing life: overcoming the impossible. For life to be fully lived, it must wrestle the impossible and win. For life to be fully lived, the God of the Impossible must be fully trusted with the writing of the script."[1]

When we say "the plot thickens," we are actually referring to the archetypal story lines, often used, that follow a prescribed course of action. There is, of course, a beginning when all is set up and the story gets moving. Then comes that plot-thickening part, made of conflict and complications accompanied by suspense and tension and resulting in a climax and final resolution or denouement.

E. M. Forster in *Aspects of the Novel* said, "A plot arranges events to reveal their significance and leads us to this question 'Why?' With a story we hear what happens; with a plot we understand."

That sounds so simplistic, clinical even. But the actual living of it is anything but simple. Jesus promised that we *will* (not might) encounter such things: "You will have suffering in this world. Be courageous! I have conquered the world" (John 16:33b).

Conflict

"This movie is really moving slowly; I keep waiting for something to happen, but it never does," Mike said to me as we watched Ismail Merchant and James Ivory's final collaboration, *The White Countess*.[2]

It starred fine actors (Ralph Fiennes and Natasha Richardson) with a somewhat interesting plot (Russian aristocracy fallen on hard times in 1930s Shanghai immediately before the Japanese invasion), but frankly there wasn't enough turmoil to make it a riveting story—one that pulled you in and never let go. Conflict is essential in good drama, and therefore we shouldn't be surprised that it's present in our lives as well.

Consider how the life story of my friend Carol Kent might have played out if not for a plot-thickening phone call several years ago. Carol, a renowned speaker and author, and her husband, Gene, were walking one day in the autumn sun near their home. "Does life ever get any better than this?" they reflected to one another, while counting their blessings of family, friends, and meaningful ministry. They were soon to find out that life indeed could get a whole lot worse.

Their only son, a strong Christian graduate of the Naval Academy, was arrested for the shooting of his wife's ex-husband. It seems Jason believed he was avenging abuse of his two young stepdaughters, and he snapped. All of a sudden this family was faced with a trial for murder. This began a several-year scenario of unending questions, legal fees, court trials, even salacious publicity on shows such as *Dateline*. And during this entire ordeal, Carol and Gene sought to find hope in seemingly hopeless circumstances.

When the verdict of guilty of first-degree murder was pronounced and the sentence of life in prison with no possibility of parole was given to this twenty-eight-year-old man, all did indeed seem hopeless. But Carol and Gene asked God to redeem this horror and help them as well as Jason to live a new script for God's kingdom. One of the first steps was Carol's brave writing of her book *When I Lay My Isaac Down: Unshakable Faith in Unthinkable Circumstances*. Another step was to start a foundation to help families of prisoners. It's called Speak Up for Hope, and God is already using it and them in remarkable ways both in the lives of prisoners as well as addressing important legislation.

It would be an understatement to say that Carol's, Gene's, and Jason's life stories changed dramatically. In the ensuing years Carol's spoken and written words (not to mention personal one-to-one counseling) have been used to encourage thousands of others living in their own hellish circumstances. In the process, Carol herself has been radically changed. She was always a great communicator and a friendly, compassionate person. But today her mantra is, "Broken people speak to broken people."

Because of the pain and perseverance in her life these past seven years, she is writing a new story of the rest of her life. With changing responses (meeting another mom in the prison ladies room, she didn't give Bible verses but simply agreed in anger and cried with her), Carol's resolve is to live a new kind of normal by making hope-filled choices after her own life turned upside down: "I can focus the deep passions of my heart on the injustices of the world, the pain and unfairness of life, on my fears for my son, on my disappointments and unfulfilled expectations—or I can view my situation as a piece of a much bigger production that I am not scripting. *I have the awesome privilege of playing a role in God's grand story, in a drama that does not waste sorrow. This story has a positive ending.*"[3]

I thank God for the example of my friends Gene and Carol, for their faithfulness, graciousness, and willingness to live out a difficult story on the front lines for all to see God's hand of hope. Mostly I pray for them with thanksgiving for their courage. For it takes courage to star in your life story, with all the plot twists and turns.

Courage

One of my favorite Bible verses is "The God of old is [your] dwelling place, and underneath are the everlasting arms" (Deut. 33:27a). It's comforting to envision myself falling into the arms of God, especially when I'm afraid of all that's happening around me. But lately I have looked at this verse in a new way. Have you ever experienced the everlasting arms of God underneath you? Catching you? Holding you up? Launching you out?

If you haven't, perhaps it is because you have come to the precipice of life and you now have a choice whether to retreat or launch into an unknown future. (For Carol and Gene the precipice was how to live when their only child had been sentenced to a life in prison.) Will you step off the edge of life as you know it and be upheld by the promised everlasting arms of God? Or will you retreat, lick your wounds, and close your eyes, dying inside long before your body ever gives out?

Here's what I've discovered about that verse: We will never experience those everlasting arms underneath us until we find ourselves flailing in air, desperately needing Him to hold us! It takes faith and courage to launch into that unknown place. But those who have done it attest to the fact that God's Word is true. He is there. When we think our greatest need is for *answers—Why did this happen? Where were You, God? How do I keep going?*—we realize that what we truly need is a *presence*, someone to walk with us through this dark night of the soul.

What our loving God offers us is His presence. "'Do not fear, for I have redeemed you; I have called you by your name; you are Mine. I will be with you when you pass through the waters, and [when you pass] through the rivers, they will not overwhelm you. You will not be scorched when you walk through the fire, and the flame will not burn you'" (Isa. 43:1b–2).

On September 11, 2001, in the midst of chaos and confusion, I received an e-mail with this quote by Peter Kreeft, reminding me that the incarnation of Christ was for such times when we need courage: "Jesus is there, sitting beside us in the lowest places of our lives. Are we broken? He was broken, like bread, for us. Are we despised? He was despised and rejected by men. Do we cry out that we can't take anymore? He was a man of sorrows and acquainted with grief. . . . Does he descend into all of our hells? Yes, he does. He was gassed in Auschwitz. He is sneered at in Soweto. He is mocked in Northern Ireland. He is enslaved in the Sudan. . . . Every tear we shed becomes his tear. He may not wipe them away yet, but he will . . . *God has not left us alone.* And for that, I love him."[4]

How will you find courage to live the story of your life? Perhaps we can all learn something from Steve Saint, whose plot thickened dramatically fifty years ago when his father, Nate Saint, and four other missionaries were speared to death by Auca Indians (now known as the Waodani) on a riverbank in the jungles of Ecuador. Steve was only five years old at the time, but his whole life would eventually be spent in coming to terms with this tragedy and even loving and living with the very people who killed his father. In his riveting book *End of the Spear* and in the film of the same title, Steve vividly portrayed the way a life story can be lived with courage. For soon after the killings, not only did another martyred missionary's widow, Elisabeth Elliot, go to live with the same Indians who speared her husband, but so did Steve's aunt, Rachel Saint. Both of them demonstrated courage to continue what their loved ones had sought to do—bring Christ to this primitive and violent tribe.

Years later, Steve and his young family were also invited to live with the Waodani and to help them not only spiritually but economically and developmentally as well. How easy it would have been for the Saints to say, "No thanks. We've already sacrificed enough for this cause." But they didn't. And the repercussions of their courage have not only launched the Waodani into the twenty-first century, but many of them have chosen to "believe God's carvings" and "walk God's trail."[5]

I first heard of Jim Elliot, Nate Saint, and the other missionaries when I was in my early twenties and seeking God's will for my own life story. Living in the mountains of North Carolina, I read *Through Gates of Splendor* and *Shadow of the Almighty* by Elisabeth Elliot and prayed that God would use me in a courageous way as well, whatever it took. While considering missionary work, I was immediately convicted that I needed more theological training and thus enrolled at Gordon-Conwell Theological Seminary. And, because God likes to orchestrate our lives in remarkable ways, I ended up living with then twice-widowed Elisabeth Elliot as her lodger, housekeeper, chauffeur, and typist. Every week I dusted tall Auca spears in the corner of the living room and typed parts of her current manuscript, *The Journals of Jim Elliot*.

Imagine the effect on a twenty-three-year-old to hear first-hand how another young woman met and lived with the very men who had made her a widow. I still remember Elisabeth sharing with me that Gikita told her in detail how he speared Jim and the others. His people didn't know any other life except killing strangers before strangers killed them. I couldn't imagine the courage it took for her to move into the jungle with her small daughter, Valerie. And since the world wanted to hear this sensational story, she wrote her first book. This pivotal event led Elisabeth Elliot to eventually write more than thirty books as well as speak all over the world to thousands of people in person and through her daily radio show *Gateway to Joy*. (By the way, she began each show with "You are loved with an everlasting love, and underneath are the everlasting arms.") And on a more personal note, Elisabeth also encouraged me to become a writer and speaker, but mostly to be a person who trusts in the Word of God and seeks to find God's redemptive hand in the midst of suffering.

In 2000, Steve Saint and his Waodani friends—Tementa and Mincaye—were invited to speak in Amsterdam to eleven thousand evangelists from 209 countries at a conference. After their moving testimonies, Steve confessed to the crowd that he had never been able to fully explain to the Waodani that what they had meant for evil so many years ago, God had used for good to help spread His gospel around the world. Steve then asked a favor of this vast audience: "Would you stand if you were significantly affected by the Auca story in any way?" He was totally unprepared for the response as thousands stood in thundering applause for the amazing story God had written, using such diverse and unlikely players.

Looking back at his own life story, Steve reflected,

Most movie scripts start with people at peace.
Then an offense, usually based on greed, is intro-

duced, leading to violence. The climax is the violent vengeance of the good guys against the bad guys. Guns blaze, explosions destroy, and the terminator walks into the sunset, soiled and slightly wounded, but victorious. This story started with tragedy and violence and worked from destruction to peace. It is a script too far-fetched to be believed—if it weren't true. But it is. . . . This isn't the end of the story. As long as there are players willing to accept their parts and a Master to write the script, it will go on. After all, life is a story. It just happens that Mincaye's and my chapter included the end of the spear.[6]

Character

In the epigraph with which I began this chapter, Nicole Johnson spoke of the difficulty of living in an invisible kingdom. Then she reiterated the by-product of such faithful living: "But the difficulty of it does not make us give up; it inspires us to overcome because our suffering is not wasteful. It counts for something that what we are going through is strengthening us in a way that helps us." When the plot thickens, will we allow it to take its course, making us either bitter or better? When we appropriate God's courage in our conflicts, what we end up developing is character.

Someone once said, "Character is who we are when no one is looking." I think that definition is right on target. Another put it this way, "When life squeezes you, what comes out?" Well, what comes out is your true character. That's why it's so important to develop a godly character before life squeezes, before the plot thickens. Paul, who had a few setbacks of his own, exhorted the believers in Rome to "rejoice in our afflictions, because we know that affliction produces endurance, endurance produces proven character, and proven character produces hope. This hope does not disappoint, because God's love has been poured out in our hearts through the Holy Spirit who was given to us" (Rom. 5:3–5).

Endurance produces character. But the process often leaves scars. One little boy remarked, "Scars are what you have left after you get well." They are merely souvenirs of the character being developed. I'm reminded that I always call those permanent dark spots on my cookie sheets "character." No matter how much I scrub, there remain scars from all the cooking through the years. When I was growing up, Mama always called them "character," and in the same way, most of us also carry permanent marks from hard living.

One of my favorite poets, Amy Carmichael, went so far as to say that those of us without scars could not have followed Jesus very far. Her poem "No Scar?" is a good reminder of what builds our character:

> Hast thou no scar?
>> No hidden scar on foot, or side, or hand?
>> I hear thee sung as mighty in the land,
>> I hear them hail thy bright ascendant star;
>> Hast thou no scar?

> Hast thou no wound?
>> Yet I was wounded by the archers, spent,
>> Leaned Me against a tree to die; and rent
>> By ravening beasts that compassed Me, I swooned:
>> Hast thou no wound?

> No wound? No scar?
>> Yet, as the Master shall the servant be,
>> And pierced are the feet that follow Me;
>> But thine are whole: Can he have followed far
>> Who has nor wound nor scar?[7]

Remember Susan (from chap. 5) who lost her son and yet vowed to keep speaking and singing through her Heartsong Ministries? Well, many years after that tragic event, Susan was speaking at a ladies tea and though she had no intention of sharing about her son, the Holy Spirit prodded her to mention it as part of her testimony. Afterward a woman came up to her and said that while listening she had thought to herself, *That woman has never been through a hard day in her life. I thought she couldn't possibly relate to someone like me, with my kind of pain.* Her own son had died six months before. And when she heard Susan speak of Thomas's death, she came away with a powerful word from God—*evidence.*

She turned to Susan and said, "Seeing such joy in you gave me the evidence that if God can restore your life like He has, He can and will restore mine too. I know now that my life—and even my pain—is not worthless. I know that it will take time, but I'll always remember this day as the day God planted the evidence in my heart and told me I will make it. Miss Susan, whatever you do, don't ever stop being that evidence!"[8]

What is the evidence of God's work in your life? How have circumstances shaped who you are and what your story has become? I suspect you are not where you thought you'd be by now. Twists and turns have set you on a path you may not have chosen, and you find your script is being rewritten, despite your dreams and plans. Perhaps it's time to review that wonderful promise from God, found in Jeremiah 29:11: "For I know the plans I have for you . . . plans for [your] welfare, not for disaster, to give you a future and a hope."

In the movie *Mr. Holland's Opus,* young Glenn Holland (played by Richard Dreyfus) dreams of one day writing a beautiful symphony, but instead he becomes a high school music teacher. As the years go by, he sees the death of another dream when his only child is born deaf. Not only is he not a symphonic composer, but he has to relinquish the desire for a musical family as well.

Still, throughout his life he finds joy in teaching music to high school students, even though his own teenage son seems distant. Wanting to reconcile, during one orchestral performance, Mr. Holland stops and signs the music for his deaf son and they recognize and love each other in a new way.[9] "This was not how Mr. Holland had once pictured the fulfillment of his youthful dream of becoming a symphony composer. Yet in that moment he realized he had accomplished a very important goal—learning how to love and be loved."[10]

Christian counselor Brenda Wagonner once confessed to her son that she felt her Christian life had been a bit like Mr. Holland's life:

I set out to be an ideal Christian wife and mother, teaching Bible stories and memorizing proverbs with him and his brother as they grew up, serving in the church, trying to have strong faith and raise a Christian family so we could have good lives. But in my youthful dreams I knew nothing of the heart of God or how to teach my kids about his real character—his goodness and love for us no matter what happens—since I didn't even know these things for myself.

Disappointments came. Plans got changed. We all had to find new dreams. Being blessed as a Christian was not at all like I once thought or planned or dreamed. I discovered God's grace unexpectedly through my failures instead of through my strengths; affection of other people through vulnerability instead of through perfection; and the love of my adult children through their acceptance of me as I am, rather than because I was the ideal example

I had once planned to be. I explained that for me, being blessed was about giving and receiving love.[11]

Perhaps it's time for you to release prior expectations and receive what has been allowed in your life story. Remember that nothing is wasted with God and that He is shaping and strengthening you through all the plot machinations of your story. If you can find courage in the conflict, then truly you will develop the character of Christ.

⟶ My Life Story ⟵

In *The Sacred Romance*, John Eldredge and Brent Curtis spoke of the "message of the arrows" and the profound effect past hurts have on our emerging life stories: "We cannot deny that the Arrows have struck us all, sometimes arriving in a hail of projectiles that blocked out the sun, and other times descending in more subtle flight that only let us know we were wounded years later, when the wound festered and broke."

What arrows have caused you pain and what messages did you take away as a result of that time of suffering? (E.g., arrow—never being asked on a date in high school; message—I'm ugly and no one will ever love me.)

What truth do you now know that contradicts that particular message?

When the perfect storm hit off the coast of Gloucester, Massachusetts, in November 1991, there was no time to warn boats of the impending disaster. Name a time in your life when you were suddenly capsized by a storm. Describe both the damage and the rescue in that story.

Name specific ways God has come alongside you during plot-thickening times of your life. Try to include a promise from Scripture if appropriate, and write that promise here as well.

Think of someone in your life who has wronged you in one way or another. What impact did that act have on the person you have become today? What would you say to him or her now?

We also rejoice in our afflictions,
because we know that affliction produces endurance,
endurance produces proven character, and proven character
produces hope. This hope does not disappoint,
because God's love has been poured out in our hearts
through the Holy Spirit who was given to us.
Romans 5:3–5

Chapter 8

Kingdom Come

Even the darkness will pass. Perhaps it won't pass until we do, until we are on the outside of our story, when the presence of the King in all his glory will give light to all that once was so dark and so difficult to understand, so impossible to bear. If you are tempted to turn back, may I encourage you to stay the course. Maintain your role in this important story and persevere through the suffering into the significance. The good that is worth holding on to.
Ken Gire, *The North Face of God*

Thy kingdom come. Thy will be done on earth as it is in heaven, I prayed as I sneaked a glance around Westminster Abbey and took a deep breath. It was majestic all right, and I was in awe as I thought about its historic significance. Moments before, His Royal Highness the Prince of Wales was announced and the Procession of the Collegiate Body began as we stood to sing "Glorious Things of Thee Are Spoken." I hoped Princess Diana was with him. After all, I was wearing my best Laura Ashley dress and carrying my instamatic camera, just in case.

It was July 1983, and during this visit to London I was invited to attend with my colleagues a "Service of Thanksgiving for the Life and Work of William Wilberforce." We were remembering before God the 150th anniversary of the death of this great man, great reformer, and great Christian. My bulletin provided a commemorative statement:

Firm in his faith, quickened by the experience of conversion, he found his vocation to advance the Kingdom of God not in the ordained ministry of the Church of England but as a member of Parliament deeply involved in affairs of state. We pay tribute to the extensive range of his sympathies which fuelled his prodigious and successful labours to bring an end to the repulsive evils of the slave trade in spite of the establishment opposition. We recall his deep concern to proclaim and witness Christ in all aspects of life, exemplified by the major part he played to bring reformation to the moral behaviour of this nation and thus remould the thinking of a whole generation. We pray that his example may inspire us to a like passion for justice, and equal concern for the oppressed and deprived, a sustained desire to free fallible man from tyrannies of body, mind and spirit.

Until then, Wilberforce had merely been a name in my church history classes. But as I watched Prince Charles lay a wreath in Westminster Abbey on the Wilberforce Memorial, I determined to find out more about this man who, 150 years after his death, still commanded respect from politicians and clergy alike.

Today I recall this event in my own life story. Two hundred years ago—on February 23, 1807—because of the unwavering efforts of Wilberforce and other committed abolitionists, the British parliament outlawed the slave trade throughout the British Empire. It is said that, amid the hurrahs of Parliament that day, William Wilberforce bowed his head and wept at the culmination of his long battle. This part of his own life story is beautifully portrayed in the film *Amazing Grace*,[1] which clearly shows a Christ follower helping to bring about the kingdom of God.

As a young man Wilberforce was one of forty members of Parliament (MPs) called the Independents who covenanted "not to accept a plum appointment to political office, a government pension, or the offer of hereditary peerage." And yet as years went by, only Wilberforce and one other stuck to that resolution. For his efforts, this five-foot-tall reformer became the brunt of taunts by such men as literary giant James Boswell:

I hate your little whittling sneer.

Your pert and self-sufficient leer . . .

begone, for shame,

Thou dwarf with big resounding name.[2]

But instead of lashing back at them, Wilberforce said his constant prayer was *God be merciful to me a sinner*. In the order of service from Westminster Abbey, there was a quote by him: "They charge me with fanaticism. If to be feelingly alive to the sufferings of my fellow creatures is to be a fanatic, I am one of the most incurable fanatics ever permitted to be at large."

While Wilberforce did not advocate pushing his faith onto others, he did believe that Christians should "boldly assert the cause of Christ in an age when so many who bear the name of Christian are ashamed of Him. Let them be active, useful, and generous toward others. Let them show moderation and self-denial themselves. Let them be ashamed of idleness. When blessed with wealth, let them withdraw from the competition of vanity and be modest, retiring from ostentation, and not be the slaves of fashion."[3]

One of the reasons Wilberforce's story has taken hold of twenty-first-century theatergoers is because this man stood by his convictions and sought to integrate his public life with his faith journey. My prayer is that we would be challenged to do the same in our own spheres of influence today. Isn't this truly what it means to have a role in God's kingdom story?

The Lord's Prayer asks that God's kingdom will come on earth and in heaven. The most amazing thing is that He wants us to be part of helping to bring that about! Have you thought about how your life story is furthering God's kingdom?

Even though it's been thirty years since I studied New Testament at Gordon-Conwell with Dr. Gordon Fee, I can still hear him saying, "The kingdom of God is already but not yet." How can it be both? Well, as best as I can understand, Jesus proclaimed the kingdom of God as something present in His ministry, but also as something still to come in glory. Thus the kingdom is not *either* present or future, but *both* present and future. It is the already-and-not-yet kingdom. It's already here and not yet fully here. Some pastors like to illustrate this truth using the example of an engaged couple (in some ways already committed in marriage but not legally yet) or a pregnant mother (in some ways already a mother but not yet in terms of actually holding her baby).

The core of Jesus's message was the proclamation of the coming of the kingdom of God: "Jesus went to Galilee, preaching the good news of God: 'The time is fulfilled, and the kingdom of God has come near. Repent and believe in the good news!'" (Mark 1:14–15). The English phrase "kingdom of God" translates a Greek phrase from the Gospels that refers not so much to the place where God rules as to the presence and power of God's actual rule. The kingdom or reign of God is here as God is exercising His authority on earth. Jesus taught us to pray, "Your kingdom come" (Luke 11:2b). But He also taught us to live by kingdom values and to be part of helping to bring about God's kingdom here on earth.

Max Lucado charged us to believe that we matter for God's kingdom: "The Kingdom needs you. The poor need you; the lonely need you; the church needs you. . . . the cause of God needs you. You are part of 'the overall purpose He is working out in everything and everyone.' (Eph. 1:12 MSG). The Kingdom needs you to discover and deploy your unique skill. Use it to make much out of God. Get the word out God is with us, we are not alone!"[4]

God wants followers who passionately pursue transformation from within and without. In the course of Kingdom living, we will be sorely tempted to give up, and that's why He also needs holy warriors who will be able to tenaciously hang on and triumph over the villain of our stories. And finally, each of us needs to realize that life on earth is not all the life there is for those who have chosen to follow Christ. While death is the end of one chapter, a new part of our stories is only beginning as we move into eternity.

A Passionate Pursuit

Do you pursue God with passion? Do you live each day with enthusiasm for what may enter into your story? Our word *enthusiasm* comes from the Greek, *en theos*, which means "with God." As you reflect on your life today, are you aware of being with God in every moment and every place? What about times in your life when you didn't yet know God? Can you trace His hand even then? Look back and seek to pinpoint ways that you have been with God and He with you in every season of life.

One of my favorite Bible characters is Peter, the personification of a passionate personality. During the Transfiguration, Peter was enthusiastic about wanting to build monuments in Jesus's honor, and Jesus had to tell him to tone it down. "Then Peter said to Jesus, 'Lord, it's good for us to be here!

If You want, I will make three tabernacles here: one for You, one for Moses, and one for Elijah'" (Matt. 17:4).

It was as though Peter desperately wanted to prove his loyalty and service to his Lord, but he went about it the wrong way. Can you relate to this? My family jokes that my epitaph will say, "She *meant* well." I, too, am passionate about a lot of things, but all too often I find myself saying and doing the wrong thing even with the right intentions. I need to learn how to channel my passions into a pursuit that honors God. And, like Peter, I deeply desire to be used by the Messiah to achieve grand and glorious things for His kingdom.

Peter wasn't afraid to try anything if God was in it: "'Lord, if it's You,' Peter answered Him, 'command me to come to You on the water.' 'Come!' He said. And climbing out of the boat, Peter started walking on the water and came toward Jesus. But when he saw the strength of the wind, he was afraid. And beginning to sink he cried out, 'Lord, save me!' Immediately Jesus reached out His hand, caught hold of him, and said to him, 'You of little faith, why did you doubt?'" (Matt. 14:28–31). But while Peter was fine with water-walking as long as he kept his eyes on Jesus, as soon as he looked down at the circumstances of his own reality, he began to sink.

Most convicting, perhaps, is that he was so *sure* of himself: "Peter told Him, 'Even if everyone runs away because of You, I will never run away!' 'I assure you,' Jesus said to him, 'tonight—before the rooster crows, you will deny Me three times!' 'Even if I have to die with You,' Peter told Him, 'I will never deny You!'" (Matt. 26:33–35a).

And yet we all know that on that fateful day, Peter gave in to fear and denied Christ:

> While Peter was in the courtyard below, one of the high priest's servants came. When she saw Peter warming himself, she looked at him and said, "You

also were with that Nazarene, Jesus." But he denied it: "I don't know or understand what you're talking about!" Then he went out to the entryway, and a rooster crowed. When the servant saw him again she began to tell those standing nearby, "This man is one of them!" But again he denied it. After a little while those standing there said to Peter again, "You certainly are one of them, since you're also a Galilean!" Then he started to curse and to swear with an oath, "I don't know this man you're talking about!" Immediately a rooster crowed a second time, and Peter remembered when Jesus had spoken the word to him, "Before the rooster crows twice, you will deny Me three times." When he thought about it, he began to weep. (Mark 14:66–72)

What had begun as a passionate pursuit was crumbling into miserable failure. How did this happen to someone with so much promise, passion, and charisma? How, of all people, could Peter have been the one to deny Christ, not once but three times? Current events in the church prompt many of us to ask similar questions about our own spiritual health. Right and left, we learn of outstanding Christ followers who have failed publicly. Could that happen to us? How will our life story play out as we continue to stumble and struggle along our journeys?

I believe each of us can have victory in the battle for our souls if we hold on tenaciously and persevere with a long obedience in the same direction.

A Tenacious Triumph

We don't know where Peter spent the weekend following the Crucifixion, but I suspect he felt anything but triumphant after his great failure. It must have been even more devastating because now, with his Lord dead, it appeared there would never be an opportunity to make things right again. But Jesus had other plans. And Peter was about to be offered a second chance.

Remember Mark's account of the Resurrection? The angel startled Mary Magdalene, Mary the mother of Jesus, and Salome with the news that Christ was no longer in the tomb: "But go, tell His disciples and Peter, 'He is going ahead of you to Galilee; you will see Him there just as He told you'" (16:7). Imagine hearing the words "and Peter." Jesus definitely wanted Peter to know of His presence. And later, when Peter, while fishing yet again, saw a man on shore and recognized Christ, he dove into the sea and swam to meet Him (John 21:1–9).

But that wasn't enough, merely to be with Jesus. No, Christ was calling Peter, precisely as He calls each of us, to persevere. I believe He actually gave Peter three opportunities to affirm his love by asking him three separate times if he truly loved Him: "When they had eaten breakfast, Jesus asked Simon Peter, 'Simon, son of John, do you love Me more than these?' 'Yes, Lord,' he said to Him, 'You know that I love You.' 'Feed My lambs,' He told him. A second time He asked him, 'Simon, son of John, do you love Me?' 'Yes, Lord,' he said to Him, 'You know that I love You.' 'Shepherd My sheep,' He told him. He asked him the third time, 'Simon, son of John, do you love Me?' Peter was grieved that He asked him the third time, 'Do you love Me?' He said, 'Lord, You know everything! You know that I love You.' 'Feed My sheep,' Jesus said" (John 21:15–17).

And Peter did. He fed sheep. He called people to repentance at Pentecost: "Repent," Peter said to them, "and be baptized, each of you, in the name of Jesus the Messiah for the forgiveness of your sins, and you will receive the gift of the Holy Spirit. For the promise is for you and for your children, and for all who are far off, as many as the Lord our God will call." And with many other words he testified and strongly urged them, saying, "Be saved from this corrupt generation!" (Acts 2:38–40).

And he spent his life story fulfilling the role God had for him. Earlier Jesus had asked Simon, "Who do you say that I am?" Simon Peter answered, "You are the Messiah, the Son of the living God!" And Jesus responded, "Simon son of Jonah, you are blessed. . . . And I also say to you that you are Peter, and on this rock I will build My church, and the forces of Hades will not overpower it. I will give you the keys of the kingdom of heaven" (Matt. 16:15–19a).

God changed Simon's name, and his new name, Peter, symbolized the role he would play out in God's story—the rock, the foundation of the church. Peter's whole life was devoted to the already-but-not-yet Kingdom. It is said that Peter came to Rome in AD 64 to help Paul with the church during Nero's persecution of the early Christians. While Paul was beheaded, Peter was crucified upside down in the Circus of Nero where the Vatican now stands. It is said he requested this position because he did not consider himself worthy to die in the same manner as his Lord Jesus Christ.

Peter persevered and continually called others to come to Christ, the living Cornerstone of God's temple: "You yourselves, as living stones, are being built into a spiritual house for a holy priesthood to offer spiritual sacrifices acceptable to God through Jesus Christ" (1 Pet. 2:5). "If we are to be living stones . . . then Peter's story must in some sense become our story. Only then will our story become like Peter's, the story of Jesus."[5]

With which part of Peter's story do you identify? The pride? The passion? The denial? The second chance? The boldness? I personally appreciate the way Peter kept going regardless of his failure, faltering, and fears. Perhaps he knew he was playing the role of a lifetime in a story that really mattered. If you believed that for yourself today, would you also keep going? Would you pick yourself up, dust yourself off, and plunge headlong into life with all its risks?

In recent years many people have been introduced to the British author J. R. R. Tolkien through the movie versions of his *Lord of the Rings* trilogy. Throughout this epic adventure there is much darkness and suffering, but there is also perseverance and determination that good will win over evil. In the second film, *The Lord of the Rings: The Two Towers*, the hobbit Frodo (Elijah Wood) and his trusted companion Sam (Sean Astin) have been climbing narrow and seemingly endless stairs cut into a mountain. They have been a long way and still have a long way to go. Frodo, tired, hungry, and thirsty, breaks down and tells Sam he can't continue.

"I know," said Sam, his face softening with his tone. "It's all wrong. By rights we shouldn't even be here. But we are. It's like in the great stories, Mr. Frodo. The ones that really mattered. Full of darkness and danger, they were. And sometimes you didn't want to know the end. Because how could the end be happy? How could the world go back to the way it was when so much bad happened? But in the end, it's only a passing thing, this shadow. Even the darkness must pass. A new day will come. And when the sun shines, it will shine out the clearer. Those were the stories that stayed with you, that meant something. Even if you were too small to understand why. But I think, Mr. Frodo, I do understand. I know now. Folk in those stories had lots of chances for turning back, only they didn't. Because they were holding on to something."

"What are we holding on to, Sam?"

"That there's some good in the world, Mr. Frodo.
And it's worth fighting for."[6]

As you consider your own journey today, do you feel like giving up or turning back? What are you holding on to? Truth that God who created you will also be the One to sustain you and guide you to journey's end? That there is good worth fighting for?

Wilberforce himself struggled with quitting the seemingly hopeless campaign but often reread a letter from John Wesley spurring him on: "Unless God has raised you up for this very thing, you will be worn out by the opposition of men and devils. But if God be for you, who can be against you? Are all of them together stronger than God? Oh, be not weary of well doing. Go on in the name of God and in the power of His might."[7] So Wilberforce continued to fight for twenty years until the slave trade was finally outlawed. And then he fought another twenty-five years, despite failing health, for the emancipation of all slaves in 1833. The battle had taken forty-six years!

Take heart in this promise from long ago: "But those who trust in the LORD will renew their strength; they will soar on wings like eagles; they will run and not grow weary; they will walk and not faint" (Isa. 40:31). You, too, can be tenaciously triumphant!

The End . . . The Beginning

We think of death as the end to our story. But for those who follow Christ, death is both an end and a beginning. Martin Luther illustrated this in "A Sermon on Preparing to Die," in which he, among other things, pointed out "The death of the dear saints is called a new birth, and their feast day is known in Latin as *natale*, that is, the day of their birth."[8]

John, in Revelation 21 and 22, spoke not only of endings but also beginnings and said that God is part of both: "I saw a new heaven and a new earth. . . . [God] will wipe all tears from their eyes, and there will be no more death, suffering, crying, or pain. These things of the past are gone forever. . . . I am making everything new. . . . I am Alpha and Omega, the beginning and the end" (21:1, 4–6 CEV).

Think of the endings to some of your favorite stories. In the movie *Titanic,* for instance, there is a grand completion of a life story. Rose, who as a young girl survived the sinking of the *Titanic* but lost her true love, has now come to the end of her life. Cameras pan over the wreck of the *Titanic* today resting on the bottom of the ocean. Slowly the ship seems to return to life in 1912 as we hear distant waltz music and see the grand staircase lit by glowing chandeliers. The movie script plays it out for us: "The music is vibrant now, and the room is populated by men in tie and tails, women in gowns. It is exquisitely beautiful. The crowd of beautiful gentlemen and ladies turns as we descend the staircase toward them. At the bottom a man stands with his back to us. . . . He turns and it is Jack (Leonardo DiCaprio). Smiling, he holds his hand out toward us. Rose (Kate Winslet) goes into his arms, a girl of seventeen. The passengers, officers, and crew of the RMS *Titanic* smile and applaud in the utter silence of the abyss."[9]

Is this what heaven will be like? Everyone in our story coming together for a final reunion? I believe in life after death, that God will finally lift the veil from our eyes and we will be able to see clearly for the first time, to understand what all His promises meant and how our stories had meaning and purpose. Fellow daughter-of-the-King Nicole Johnson pictured it this way: "The princesses will join the King. I can see us gathering around, His ragtag band of daughters, called out and named by Him, loved by the Prince, and secure in the ending. Stories to tell, griefs to share, joys to celebrate. Some of us are walking, others limping, and some leaping. Though we are scarred and maimed from our trials and battles, though we are weary and wounded, we are more beautiful than ever, anticipating living out the grandest happily ever after of all time."[10]

But perhaps the ending/beginning of our life stories is most beautifully described by C. S. Lewis at the end of his *Chronicles of Narnia* in which he brings everyone together in the closing of book 7, *The Last Battle*. Peter, Edmund, Lucy and all the others go "further up and further in," where they see Aslan the Lion who has been the Christ figure throughout the series. As all gather around in a grand reunion, he leaps down the mountain to greet them:

There was a real railway accident. Your father and mother and all of you are—as you used to call it in the Shadowlands—dead. The term is over: the holidays have begun. The dream is ended: this is the morning! And as He spoke He no longer looked to them like a lion; but the things that began to happen after that were so great and beautiful that I cannot write them. And for us this is the end of all the stories, and we can most truly say that they all lived happily ever after. But for them it was only the beginning of the real story. All their life in this world and all their adventures in Narnia had only been the cover and title page: Now at last they were beginning Chapter One of the Great Story which no one on earth has read: which goes on for ever: in which every chapter is better than the one before.[11]

During this year's Ash Wednesday service, my minister husband, using the ashes from last year's burned palm branches, made the sign of the cross on my forehead: "From dust you are, to dust you shall return, repent and believe the good news." He was tearful as he said this to me, his wife. Perhaps it is because we are getting older and both comprehend the solemnity of those words. Perhaps it is because he already lost one wife to death—twenty-six years ago. Or perhaps it is because he knows that today is the funeral of my friend Janice Chaffee.

Janice—beautiful, bright, and a marvelous teller of stories—chronicled her last three years living with multiple myeloma. She wrote long letters describing not only treatments but also how she was processing and feeling throughout the ordeal. Because she lived in Nashville and I'm near Hartford, we rarely saw each other, but we did connect in person about seven months ago when she surprised our group of fellow authors at our annual conference. What joy to embrace her tiny frame and talk with her of future dreams. And how special to hear that she and her husband, Jim, and their sons had recently finished filming a project with the A&E Network. I haven't seen the documentary yet, but it is about dying. Perhaps more importantly, it is about living. And Janice and Jim, strong to the end, were perfect subjects to lift up the hope that life as we know it is not all there is.

The reason I loved Janice and loved her writing was because she believed in the connectedness of stories and went out of her way to share those stories of redemption and reconciliation. Her books *Sisters: The Story Goes On, One Silent Night,* and *If the Prodigal Were a Daughter* all contained stories for hope and healing. "Telling our stories reveals who we are," Janice often said. "Our stories offer hope and instruction to those who listen." She based the importance and necessity of telling stories on the example of Jesus, the greatest storyteller of all time.

The last time I heard from her was shortly before Christmas, as she was preparing to celebrate the third anniversary of her diagnosis:

> How life has changed during the past 36 months. I've endured more than I thought possible, laughed until I cried and cried until no tears were left. Some things are drastically different: my body, my perspective, my sense of what's important. Some things have not changed: my love for Jim and Elliott and Taylor; my faith that God is present, my belief that we are all sufferers on a journey toward perfection of character and soul. I'm paying close attention to the journey. Annie Dillard once wrote something like this, "The way we live this day, how we lived this hour, is how we live our lives." "To the fullest" is my daily, hourly goal and that is my wish for you . . . that "to the fullest" you will enjoy the merriest of Christmases and the Happiest of New Years.[12]

In her song "The Story Goes On" Janice gave a charge to all of us:

> And the story goes on
> The weak are made strong
> Each time it's told others find hope
> And the story goes on.
>
> We are all living proof
> Of the power of truth
> And one by one we pass it along
> The story goes on.[13]

Though Janice is no longer here on earth, her story does go on. Shortly before her death, Jim wrote about his own story: "I have never envisioned my life script beyond Janice, so for right now I hear the click of keys daring to write a new chapter in the Chaffee story but I refuse to budge from the pages we presently share. This has to make sense to many of you. Janice and I drink every ounce of time we have left together. These last three years, as horrifying as they often have been have also been a great gift to us both. We have had the opportunity to live life as very few do, with a clear view of what is really important, what really matters. . . . So we will take weeks, months or whatever time we have . . . and we will live our lives as God intended for us to live, this moment, this day. Is this not, in fact, how we all should live?"[14]

Will you live, as Jim says, "as God intended for us to live, *this* moment, *this* day?" And what will your legacy be? A legacy isn't only a monetary inheritance; it is something far more. My own legacy will be whatever part of my story others remember about me after I'm gone. And, if our children are the gift we give to a world we will never see, then the footprints I leave for my four children—Justin, Tim, Fiona, and Maggie—become an important focus of my life.

The Southern author William Faulkner once remarked that there was a big difference between leaving monuments and leaving footprints: "A monument says 'At least I got this far.' While a footprint says 'This is where I was when I moved again.'"[15] Most of us will not have monuments erected in our memory when our lives are over. But all of us can leave footprints for others to follow.

The great adventurer Norman Vaughan died recently at age one hundred. While he didn't leave a monument, there is a mountain in the South Pole named for him. In 1929 Norman Vaughan was the dog handler for Admiral Richard Byrd's expedition to Antarctica. It was an arduous task and very dangerous, but it was successful, and Vaughan promised himself that someday he would return to climb his name-sake mountain.

And he did return in 1994, but by that time he was eighty-nine years old with a bad knee and a weak ankle. The thirty-degree slope he remembered was actually forty degrees. It would take him eight days to climb up and one day down. But instead of being defeated, he decided to accept the challenge and let it push him forward. He also had lots of help; 7,129 footsteps were cut for him in the snow by fellow climbers so he could ascend Mount Vaughan.[16]

In your life story, how many of God's people have carved footsteps so you might know the path and find sure footing—so you might not give up? Because of the body of Christ, the church community, and because of God's utter faithfulness, shall we keep walking the journey of faith, even as we stumble and get redirected, trusting that even our faltering footprints will somehow be part of furthering God's kingdom?

God has called you to live the role of a lifetime as part of His grand story. Will you accept your role and live it fully, following your Director and playing only to an audience of One? This is my deepest prayer for my own life story. That I may live in such a way that on that day when I go "further up and further in" I'll be welcomed with the words, "Well done, good and faithful servant."

> Oh, may all who come behind us find us faithful.
> May the fire of our devotion light their way.
> May the footprints that we leave,
> lead them to believe
> and the lives we live inspire them to obey.
> Oh, may all who come behind us find us faithful.
>
> —Jon Mohr[17]

— My Life Story —

What well-known person's death (in your own lifetime) did you grieve most and why?

When I was a seminary student, I had the assignment of writing my own obituary. It was very sobering and definitely provided perspective. If you were to die tomorrow, what would your obituary say? Write it here.

Winston Churchill left instructions for "Taps" to be played at his funeral, immediately followed by a rousing rendition of "Reveille." This was to point out that death is both an end and a beginning.

Consider your own funeral. List participants, Scripture, music, and other elements you would like to have included when the time comes. Perhaps there is an office at your church where such files are kept for future reference. If not, be sure to give this list to your closest relative. Try to approach this exercise as a way of celebrating your life rather than thinking of a dreaded death.

Judaism supports the tradition of leaving an ethical will as part of a spiritual legacy. What would you like to write as part of your own spiritual legacy for those you leave behind? Here's a guideline (from Jewish Lights Publishing) to follow, but I encourage you to design your own:

Opening
  "I write this to you, my . . ."
  "In order to . . ."

The family
  My parents, siblings, relatives were/are . . .
  Events that helped shape our family . . .

Religious observances/insights
  The rituals of most meaning to me . . .
  Specific teachings from values and spiritual sources that move me most . . .

Personal history
  People who strongly influenced my life . . .
  Events which helped shape my life . . .

Ethical ideas and practices
  Ideas that found expression in my life . . .
  "I would like to suggest to you the following . . ."

Closing
  "My ardent wishes for you . . ."
  "May the Almighty God . . ."

Are you living today the way you want to be remembered tomorrow? What about the way you spend time? Your priorities? Your relationships?

Target one change you could make in each of those areas, with God's help, so you can truly live your legacy. Don't wait!

I saw a new heaven and a new earth. . . .
[God] will wipe all tears from their eyes, and there will be
no more death, suffering, crying, or pain. These things of the
past are gone forever. . . . I am making everything new. . . .
I am Alpha and Omega, the beginning and the end.
Revelation 21:1, 4–6 CEV

Epilogue

Warrior Princess

That eight-year-old princess has now traded in her sparkling tiara for a glittering brooch, what the kids would definitely refer to as "bling." It is a large rhinestone sword overlaid with a large rhinestone crown—a gift from my friend Gail. I admit it's definitely an in-your-face piece of jewelry. But I wear it proudly to remember my role in God's story. Gail told me, "Wear your crown because you are a royal daughter all glorious within the palace. Take up your sword and understand that you walk in God's power. Wear them both and always remember, you are a daughter of the King!"

I am a warrior princess.

I am a daughter of the King of kings. And I am called to fight in the battle between good and evil, truth and treachery. All other roles are eclipsed by this primary focus. The battle cry I respond to is everything from Esther's "I shall go to the King and if I perish, I perish" to Narnia's "Further up and further in." From Susan Duke's "You've made the wrong mama mad!" to Larry Walters's "You can't just sit there!" From Martin Luther's "We will not fear for God hath willed His truth to triumph through us!" to Isaiah's "Here I am, send me!" Or from Steve Saint's "This isn't the end of the story!"

to John Wesley's "Go on in the name of God and in the power of His might."

What is your battle cry today? What will cause you to dig deep and summon all resources to launch forward into the life story God has planned for you—full of drama and discouragement, daring and delight? Whatever it takes, go for it. Today is the only opportunity you have. Don't miss your life!

In a scene from *The Lord of the Rings: the Return of the King*, the returning king—Aragorn (Viggo Mortensen)—on his horse, is rallying the horsemen behind him against the forces of evil. His men are greatly outnumbered by the evil Orcs, and the battle seems hopeless. But when Aragorn speaks, he becomes the king—the role he was always called to play in this grand epic. He calls to his comrades, "I see in your eyes the same fear that would take the heart of me." He pauses for a moment, then continues with renewed vigor. "A day may come when the courage of men fails, when we forsake our friends and break all bonds of fellowship." Then standing tall in his saddle, he shouts, "But it is not *this* day! This day we fight! By all that you hold dear on this good earth—I bid you stand!" And with those words he leads the charge against the enemy, with ultimate triumph.[1]

I know that life is difficult, and it's inevitable that a day may come when we simply feel we cannot take it any longer. One day our courage may fail. One day we may forsake friends, fellowship, and faith. But, dear princesses and princes, may it not be *this* day! This day we fight! This day we live our life story, fulfilling the unique role God has for us in His kingdom. May we live well with integrity and honor because our story truly matters to God and to those who come behind us.

The kingdom of this world has become
the kingdom of our Lord, and of His Christ;
and He shall reign for ever and ever.
King of Kings, and Lord of Lords.
Hallelujah! Amen!
—George Frideric Handel ~ *Messiah*

THE END. . . . THE BEGINNING. . . .

Acknowledgments

This book was written with the help of a cast of thousands! Well, not really, but the truth is, I have been influenced by every person who has touched my life (and that probably is a cast of thousands!). Special thanks and bouquets to:

- All my wonderful friends and colleagues at B&H Publishing Group in Nashville, especially my editor Leonard Goss, for believing in me and urging me to go "further up and further in" every day.

- Other authors who inspired and supported me: Lael Arrington, Virelle Kidder, Jeanne Zornes, Carol Kent, Nancy McGuirk, Linda Johnson, Pam Palagyi, and Maggie Rowe. A special thanks to my daily support group of Awesome AWSAs—the Advanced Writers and Speakers Association—especially 2007 AWSA of the Year, the late Janice Chaffee. Truly you are sisters who know what my life is like.

- Gracious people who provided special "apart" places to remember, write, and create: Monty and Anne Ortman (Anacortes, Washington); Don and Judy Jordan (Singing Hills, New Hampshire); the Waterses, Singleterys, and Feinbergs (Thomasville, Georgia);

and the Sonjus and Hammonds (Camp of the Woods, New York).

- Two actors both named Maggie—Maggie McDowell and Maggie Rowe—who are a great source for all things theatrical and dramatic. Hope I got all the metaphors right in this book!
- My "Daybreak" prayer/birthday/spa group—Judy Franzen, Karen Memmott, and Jessica Parchman. Also, the prayer support from my home church family—First Church of Christ Congregational in Wethersfield, Connecticut.
- Girlz4God, my weekly teen Bible study who prayed so hard for Mrs. McDowell "to get that book contract" and then "to finish her book by the deadline." God did it, girls!
- A friend from my backstory—Claire Whitfield Tucker—who has graciously reentered my life with encouragement and memories.
- Spellbinding storytellers such as Walter Wangerin Jr., Karen Mains, Max Lucado, Becky Pippert, Ken Gire, Elisabeth Elliot, Steve Brown, Anne Lamott, Michael Card, Maggie Rowe, and Patricia Raybon.
- My favorite storyteller of all time—Pratt Secrest. Thanks, Daddy, for inspiring and encouraging me to live out my role of a lifetime. You are my hero forever!
- My mama, Sarah Secrest, for your unending support and strength in every season of life. And all the other girls in my family who cheer me on and keep me humble too—sisters Cathy Secrest Ray and Susan Secrest Waters; sisters-in-law Tracey McDowell Plath, Roxanne McDowell Robison, Annelies Orechkoff, Asti Van Veen, and Joann Van Seventer; and special Aunt Carol Singletery.

- My four children who are definitely the most committed, outstanding, and grace-filled gang a mama could ever hope for! Justin, your courage and perseverance every single day inspire me to no end; truly you are an overcomer. Tim, I love and appreciate your spontaneity and regular phone calls (from three thousand miles away) urging me to live one day at a time—with gusto! Fiona, thanks for being home awhile in between living on two other continents; your heart for those in need is inspiring and challenging, and I appreciate your trying to keep me grounded. And Maggie Sarah, I can't even imagine next year without you, but know that wherever you are and whatever role you assume, I'm your biggest fan and greatest supporter all the way!

- My husband of twenty-three years, Michael McDowell. Honey, without you my life story might have been dull, predictable, lonely, normal, quiet, ordinary, and forgettable. With you as my life partner, I have the privilege of facing each day with anticipation at how God will show His faithfulness in both our lives as we trust Him for grace, guidance, and glory. I love you the world!

- Jesus Christ, Lover of my soul and Lifter of my head, truly I am amazed that You deign to offer me a role in Your story of the Kingdom with no end. I'm responding with a big "Yes" as I remain Yours—always—under the mercy . . .

Lucinda Secrest McDowell
Gracehaven
Wethersfield, Connecticut
May 2007

Notes

Chapter 1

1. Madeleine L'Engle, *Walking on Water: Reflections on Faith and Art* (Colorado Springs: Shaw Publishers, 2001).

2. Steven Curtis Chapman and Scotty Smith, *Restoring Broken Things* (Brentwood, TN: Integrity Publishers, 2005), 18.

3. *Walk the Line*, James Mangold, director and screenplay (Twentieth Century Fox, 2005); Johnny Cash and Gill Dennis, book.

4. *Hartford Courant*, August 2006, www.courant.com.

5. David Sper, *The Greatest Story Ever Told* (Grand Rapids, MI: RBC Ministries, 1999), 2.

6. John Eldredge, *Epic* (Nashville, TN: Thomas Nelson, 2004), 12–13.

7. Dale Tolmasoff, *This Is No Fairy Tale* (Wheaton, IL: Crossway, 2005), 10.

8. Frederick Buechner, *A Room Called Remember* (New York: HarperCollins, 1984), 49ff.

Chapter 2

1. David V. Andersen, "When God Adopts," *Christianity Today*, 19 July 1993, 36.

2. *The Princess Diaries*, Garry Marshall, director, and Gina Wendkos, screenplay (Bottom of the Ninth Productions, 2001); Meg Cabot, book.

3. Andrea Stephens, *Girlfriend, You Are a B.A.B.E.: Beautiful, Accepted, Blessed and Eternally Significant* (Grand Rapids, MI: Revell, 2005).

4. Jan Coleman, *The Woman Behind the Mask* (Grand Rapids, MI: Kregel, 2005), 22.

5. *Simon Birch*, Mark Steven Johnson, director and screenplay (Caravan Pictures, 1998); John Irving, book.

6. Max Lucado, *Cure for the Common Life* (Nashville, TN: Thomas Nelson, 2005), 171.

7. Ibid., 163–64.

8. *Chronicles of Narnia: The Lion, the Witch and the Wardrobe*, Andrew Adamson, director; Andrew Adamson, Ann Peacock, Christopher Markus, and Stephen McFeely, screenplay (Walt Disney Pictures, 2005); C. S. Lewis, book.

9. Andrew and Kate Adamson, *The Lion, the Witch and the Wardrobe: The Movie Storybook* (HarperEntertainment, 2005), 135.

10. *One Night with the King*, Michael O. Saibel, director, and Stephan Blinn, screenplay (Gener8Xion Entertainment, 2006); Mark Andrew Olsen and Tommy Tenney, book.

Chapter 3

1. Royal B. C. Museum in Victoria, British Columbia, Canada, www.royal bcmuseum.com.

2. Dan B. Allender, *To Be Told* (Colorado Springs, CO: WaterBrook, 2005), 1, 3.

3. Dan B. Allender and Lisa K. Fann, *To Be Told Workbook* (Colorado Springs, CO: WaterBrook, 2005), 50.

4. Richard L. Morgan, *Remembering Your Story* (Nashville, TN: Upper Room Books, 2002), 32.

5. Ibid., 33.

6. Lucinda Secrest McDowell, *Quilts from Heaven: Parables from the Patchwork of Life* (Nashville, TN: B&H Publishing Group, 2007), 38. To order a signed copy of this full-color, hardback book, send $17 to Encouraging Words that Transform, P.O. Box 290707, Wethersfield, CT 06129.

7. For more on the subject of how grace radically changes lives, see Lucinda Secrest McDowell, *Amazed by Grace* (Quiet Waters Publishers, 2002). To order a signed copy, send $18 to Encouraging Words that Transform, P.O. Box 290707, Wethersfield, CT 06129.

Chapter 4

1. "GenNexters," www.pewresearch.org/databank

2. www.wikipedia.org/wiki/Famous_for_being_famous

3. "Who Are Your Heroes?," www.berkeley.edu/news/media/release, 11 May 2006.

4. *The Holiday*, Nancy Meyers, director and writer (Columbia Pictures, 2006).

5. C. S. Lewis, "The Weight of Glory," sermon. Church of Saint Mary the Virgin, Oxford, England, 8 June 1942; published in *Theology*, November 1941, and by the S.P.C.K., 1942.

6. *Stranger Than Fiction*, Marc Forster, director, and Zach Helm, writer (Crick Pictures LLC, 2006).

7. Lael Arrington, *Godsight* (Wheaton, IL: Crossway, 2005), 150 and 157.

8. Ibid., 154.

9. Gary Haugen, "When the Will of God Is Scary," *Fuller Seminary Magazine*, Winter 2007, 31.

10. Ibid., 31.

11. Eric and Leslie Ludy, *When God Writes Your Life Story* (Sisters, OR: Multnomah, 2004), 98.

Chapter 5

1. *The Passion of the Christ*, Mel Gibson, director; Benedict Fitzgerald and Mel Gibson, writers (Icon Productions, 2004).

2. Arrington, *Godsight*, 137.

3. Susan Duke, *Grieving Forward* (New York: Warner Faith, Hachette Book Group, 2006), 12.

4. Ibid., 13.

5. Joanna Weaver, *Having a Mary Spirit* (Colorado Springs, CO: WaterBrook, 2006), 27.

6. Eldredge, *Epic*, 100.

7. Ken Gire, *The North Face of God* (Wheaton, IL: Tyndale, 2005), 195.

Chapter 6

1. *Indiana Jones and the Last Crusade*, Steven Spielberg, director, and Jeffrey Boam, screenplay (Lucasfilm, 1989); George Lucas, story.

2. Vinita Hampton Wright, *The Soul Tells a Story* (Downers Grove, IL: InterVarsity, 2005), 168.

Chapter 7

1. Ludy, *When God Writes Your Life Story*, 21.

2. *The White Countess*, James Ivory, director, and Kazuo Ishiguro, writer (Merchant Ivory Productions, 2006).

3. Carol Kent, *When I Lay My Isaac Down* (Colorado Springs, CO: NavPress, 2004), 165.

4. Peter Kreeft, "What Is God's Answer to Human Suffering?" quoted from *Making Sense Out of Suffering* by Peter Kreeft (Ignatius Press), www. peterkreeft.com.

5. *End of the Spear*, Jim Hanon, director, and Bill Ewing, Bart Gavigan, and Jim Hanon, writers (Every Tribe Entertainment, 2006).

6. Steve Saint, *End of the Spear* (Wheaton, IL: Tyndale House, 2005), 331.

7. Amy Carmichael, *Toward Jerusalem* (Fort Washington, PA: Christian Literature Crusade, 1936), 85.

8. Duke, *Grieving Forward*, 182.

9. *Mr. Holland's Opus*, Stephen Herek, director, and Patrick Sheane Duncan, writer (Hollywood Pictures, 1996).

10. Brenda Waggoner, *Fairy Tale Faith* (Wheaton, IL: Tyndale, 2003), 189–90.

11. Ibid.

Chapter 8

1. *Amazing Grace*, Michael Apted, director, and Steven Knight, writer (Walden Media, 2007).

2. Marvin Olasky, "Humble Courage," *World*, 10 February 2007, 44.

3. Ibid., 44.

4. Lucado, *Cure for the Common Life*, 68.

5. Michael Card, *The Fragile Stone* (Downers Grove, IL: InterVarsity, 2003), 186.

6. *The Lord of the Rings: The Two Towers*, Peter Jackson, director, and Fran Walsh, screenplay (New Line Cinema, 2002); J. R. R. Tolkien, book.

7. Charles Colson, "The Perseverance of Wilberforce," *Breakpoint* commentary, 23 February 2007.

8. Dennis Ngien, "Picture Christ," *Christianity Today*, April 2007, vol. 51, no. 4, 69.

9. *Titanic*, James Cameron, director and writer (Twentieth Century Fox, 1997).

10. Nicole Johnson, *Keeping a Princess Heart* (Nashville, TN: Thomas Nelson, 2003), 181.

11. C. S. Lewis, *The Last Battle* (New York: Penguin Books, 1956), 165.

12. A letter from Janice Chaffee, December 20, 2006, used by permission. Order her books from www.janicechaffee.com.

13. Janice Chaffee, Ty Lacy, Connie Harrington, "The Story Goes On," 1995, Word Music, ASCAP/Shepherd's Fold Music (BMI) (Administrated by Reunion Music Publishers) ASCAP. All rights reserved. Used by permission. www.janicechaffee.com.

14 A letter from Jim Chaffee, January 29, 2007, used by permission. www.janicechaffee.com.

15. William Faulkner, *The Town* (Random House, 1957).

16. Norman Vaughan, *My Life of Adventure* (Stackpole Books, 1995).

17. Jon Mohr, "Find Us Faithful," Birdwing Music, 1987.

Epilogue

1. *The Lord of the Rings: The Return of the King*, Peter Jackson, director, and Fran Walsh, screenplay (New Line Cinema, 2003); J. R. R. Tolkien, book.

About the Author

Lucinda Secrest McDowell has been a storyteller all her life. Her greatest joy is to make God's faithfulness visible and real through practical illustrations of biblical truth in ordinary life. Cindy does this through her writing and speaking ministry, Encouraging Words that Transform! A graduate of Gordon-Conwell Theological Seminary and Furman University, she also studied at the Wheaton Graduate School of Communication. Cindy has authored six other books, including *Spa for the Soul, Quilts from Heaven, Amazed by Grace,* and *What We've Learned So Far.* She is a contributing author to twenty other books and has been published in more than fifty magazines.

In addition to reading, watching and sharing stories, Cindy enjoys tea parties, letters on fine stationery, cozy quilts, massage, country music, bright colors, and laughing friends. She has spent the past sixteen years living in a New England village with her husband and four children.

Her life verse (adopted in 1971) is Isaiah 58:10–11: *"If you spend yourselves in behalf of the hungry and satisfy the needs of the oppressed, then your light will rise in the darkness, and your night will become like the noonday. The* LORD *will guide you always; he will satisfy your needs in a sun-scorched land and will strengthen your frame. You will be like a well-watered garden, like a spring whose waters never fail"* (NIV).

Cindy has no idea where and how the rest of her life story will unfold.

For information on books and speaking,
please contact her at:
Encouraging Words that Transform!
P.O. Box 290707
Wethersfield, CT 06129 USA
Phone: (860) 257-WORD
E-mail: cindy@encouragingwords.net
Web site: www.EncouragingWords.net